"Ever wonder what kind of people helped build NPI
tution it is today? Peter Breslow's rollicking memoir
it took to make radio from the farthest reaches of the ̄.... ....... .......
Mt. Everest with his sound equipment). Peter's life is one wild adventure after
another and we lucky readers get to go along for the ride."

**—RACHEL MARTIN**, NPR Host

"Peter takes us on a wild ride of assignments from the South Pole to the Amazon
to Mogadishu to Baghdad, and also prompts a rattlesnake to spit venom on his
microphone. His memorable memoir takes us behind the scenes of some of the
most important events of our times. It also tells how NPR grew from a fledgling
network into a major news source, and how a Jersey Boy traveled the world and
became a widely respected journalist."

**—SCOTT SIMON**, host NPR's *Weekend Edition Saturday*

"I'm so glad I'm not Peter Breslow's mother. I'd worry myself to pieces. The der-
ring-dos on these pages had me scared, impressed, laughing, fretting. And that's
just the first chapter. He's seen most of the world, often under the worst circumstances, and could navigate it all with humor and smarts. Never heard of a Bad
Boy Eagle Scout until I met him. So glad I did."

**—SUSAN STAMBERG**, NPR Special Correspondent

"Bravely willing to go wherever the most compelling stories take him, seemingly
oblivious to inconvenience and personal danger, producer Peter Breslow has long
been a rock star of radio journalism. Diehard fans of NPR have been listening to
his excellent work for decades without knowing it. In this crisply-written and often
hilarious memoir, Breslow takes us from political hot spots to natural disasters to
war zones, and literally around the planet—including its rooftop (Everest) and
its basement (Antarctica). Along the way, he gives us an enticing peek into the
vibrant world of radio journalism that exists beyond the editing suites and studio
microphones." **—HAMPTON SIDES**, *New York Times* bestselling author of
*Ghost Soldiers*, *Blood and Thunder*, and *On Desperate Ground*

"In radio, there is something called a "driveway moment"—a story so good you
stay in your car to listen even if you've arrived at your home. Peter Breslow's book
is packed with dozens of driveway moments—or whatever is the literary equivalent (not-turning-off the-light-and-going-to-sleep-even-though-it's-midnight
moments?) What a feast of stories! You'll read about ping-pong-playing Central
American revolutionaries, televangelists, political prisoners in Iraq, and trips to
the Arctic circle without food. All of the tales are told with Peter's wit, introspec-
tion and warmth. Plus, if you are interested in a career in radio, this book is a must-
read. But regardless of your profession, you'll be enthralled by the adventures."

**—A.J. JACOBS**, *New York Times* bestselling author of
*The Year of Living Biblically*

# Outtakes

———

## Stumbling Around the World for NPR

———

Peter Breslow

MOJO HAND PUBLISHING

Cover and book design by Mark Melnick

Published by
MOJO HAND PUBLISHING

For Jessica, Eden, Danielle . . . and Sadie

NO. 0726

# NEWS MEDIA

PETER BRESLOW

NATIONAL PUBLIC RADIO

**METROPOLITAN POLICE DEPARTMENT**
District of Columbia

*Luck is a very thin wire between survival and disaster and not many people can keep their balance on it.*

HUNTER S. THOMPSON

# PRESS

National Public Radio®

1111 N. Capitol St. NE

Washington, DC 20002

202-513-2000

#34895

**Peter Breslow**

Employee Name

Signature

National Public Radio, Inc

Expiration Date
17 Nov 2014

# Contents

# Room Tone

I am sitting in a room with a head of state, a famous alt rocker, a Nobel laureate, a Hollywood superhero or maybe even an Afghan warlord. We are almost knee to knee, not making a sound. It is so utterly quiet you can hear the clock on the wall ticking. Lord, please don't let me burp or fart or have my stomach gurgle, because I am taping the longest minute in radio. I am recording room tone—the pure sound of the room.

Usually, interviewees are more than accommodating even if they don't quite get what I'm up to, but sometimes they fidget and I have to remind them to settle down. Or there is something they just have to say to their assistant. Shush!

I tell them it will only be for a minute—we need to sit here without making any noise for a minute—maybe even only 45 seconds. But they look at their watch five times, not understanding how a minute could possibly last this long. No one wants to make eye contact. If they do, there is usually just a tight smile.

Some people look at room tone as a moment of Zen—an opportunity for a mini one-minute meditation. Or perhaps they take stock of the conversation they've just had with me and decide they'd like to clarify something or make an additional point. However, if they have second thoughts about what they just said and want to strike it from the record, I will likely say no. Once they agree to the interview, it's on the record.

My eyes wander; maybe I notice a spot that the prime minister missed when he was shaving that morning, or I see that the warlord's nails are improbably manicured. Perhaps the rocker is breathing heavily—is she a smoker?

Coastal Ecuador, 2001

My mind wanders. I should get the oil changed in the Subaru this week. Is the solstice on the 20th or the 21st?

The interminable minute finally expires and everyone exhales, relieved.

Recording room tone is the essential conclusion of almost all out-of-the-studio interviews. Every room you walk into has a tone. Even if it seems absolutely quiet, there is some little noise generated by a fluorescent light, or a distant highway, or an upstairs neighbor blasting Beyonce. So once a conversation not conducted in the perfect quiet of a recording studio is over, we ask the guest to sit still for a minute so that we can tape the tone of the room.

Afterwards, when producing an audio story, we will use these 60 seconds of subtle sound during the final mix of the piece to smooth the modest difference in tone between that room and the dead silence of the studio where we record our narration. Listeners are sophisticated and their ears can detect that difference; and room tone goes a long way towards making a story sound seamless.

Sometimes you have to do a bit of work to get an office or apartment quiet enough in the first place for an interview. Too much background noise and it can make the conversation very tough to edit.

When interviewing some top government officials during a trip to Hanoi in 1989, the overhead lights in the room buzzed, so we turned them off. The small fridge in the corner hummed, so we unplugged it. We shut down the rattling air conditioners and the whooshing ceiling fans. The street outside was cacophonous with whining motorbikes, so we closed the windows in 90-degree heat. And everyone except us was chain smoking.

After 45 minutes in the sweltering dimness, our shirts were smelly and soaked through, but we got clean sounding tape. It's always about getting the best tape (even though it's not really tape anymore, just bits and bytes).

Room tone is arcane and probably to most people seemingly unnecessary. I mean, who cares if there is a slight sounding variation going from studio narration to a tape cut and back again. The people who make audio at NPR care. It is this meticulous attention to detail that makes our productions what they are and our journalism what it is.

It's worth saying again—it's always about getting the best tape.

On a Rhino Roundup in Chitwan National Park, Nepal with reporter
John Nielsen and sound engineer Bill McQuay, 2001

# Introduction

When I tell people I'm a producer at NPR, three questions invariably follow:

1. How did you get started there?
2. What's it like to work there?
3. What does a producer do anyway?

In the pages you're holding, I hope to answer these queries so completely that I will never be asked them again. But just in case you're browsing in a bookstore right now—reading this with no intention of purchasing this book—here's the short version so your afternoon will not have been a complete waste.

1. I absolutely BS-ed my way in the door at NPR with no experience, but a fair amount of chutzpah. National Public Radio had been around for only a decade or so when I showed up utterly unqualified on its doorstep looking for work. The place was still getting its journalistic sea legs, which left an opportunity for me to slip in almost unnoticed.

Now, BS might get you in the door, but ultimately you have to be able to do the work. So I kept my eyes (and ears) open, looking over the shoulders of people who, in fact, did know what they were doing and began to learn the craft of radio production. It turned out I was a pretty quick study and had a knack for it, so before anyone could check my references, I accepted the job.

Since those days, NPR has sent me up Mt. Everest and down to the South Pole, with quite a few stops in between for wars, underwater hockey and deadline hubbub. I have always tried to bring the listener along on my adventures, and that's my goal as well for you, dear reader, with the added bonus of including the behind-the-scenes skinny on how the stories were produced.

2. Working at NPR is rewarding, challenging, confounding, and fun. It has now been around long enough that some of our hosts and reporters can be included in the *Jeopardy* category, Legendary Broadcasters. Over almost 40 years—as we've gone from cutting audio tape with a razor blade to digitally editing on our computers—I have had the privilege of working with the best of the best.

They, as well as fellow producers and editors, have pushed me to do my strongest work and admonished me (usually gently) when I have fallen short. They are the most committed people I know. In this book, I will put you in the edit booth side-by-side with NPR talent as they make their audio magic.

Every week I walk in the door and face a program with a voracious appetite for quality stories. It can be a news treadmill that scarcely gives you time to catch your breath. Not all of the work is exceptional, but a great deal of it certainly is. It is also exhilarating and satisfying, especially when a story you have worked on has touched someone, helped right a wrong, or made milk shoot out of somebody's nose.

Whether it's the pressure of the deadline or the chemistry of the workplace, zaniness has been a recurring theme during my tenure at NPR. Hardly a day goes by when I don't cackle loudly at my job.

Of course, it's not idyllic. There are by-the-book managers who relish rules. There is work on the weekends, long hours, and way too many meetings. But the sense of mission permeates most of what we do.

My goal is that by the time you close this book you will feel NPR's DNA in your bones and understand what would keep a blues loving wisenheimer from New Jersey at the organization all these years.

3. What a producer does depends on many things. My father went to his sweet hereafter never truly understanding exactly what his son did for a living.

There are all kinds of producers. Some put together programs; some spend all their days editing interviews; some are basically reporters who usually don't get their voices on the air (don't get me started).

Okay, it's too late; you got me started. If you are a producer, you have to be willing to make other people, i.e. hosts and reporters, sound good while you suppress your ego for the sake of the team.

Unlike my father, when you finish reading, you will understand exactly what a producer does. You will also hear what it is like to respond to a huge breaking-news situation while you're on the air, watch helplessly as a colleague is possibly kidnapped by rebels, and have your microphone spat on by a rattlesnake. In short, you will step into the NPR kitchen and learn how the audio sausage is made.

Now, quit being such a cheapskate. Go to the cash register and pay for this book. That goes for you online browsers too.

# Chapter 1

# Early Radio Days

It's an initial round in my tryout for a production assistant position at *All Things Considered (ATC)*. We are writing scripts on typewriters, so copy changes are laborious. I'm working on an introduction to a piece for host Susan Stamberg to read. In these first days I don't own a watch, however, and I lose track of the time. All of a sudden, the producer is yelling. "Get that into the studio now!"

"But, but . . . the intro needs to be re-written."

"Now!"

I burst into the studio and run up to Susan sitting at the microphone. She is an icon. A radio goddess. The first woman to anchor a national nightly news program. And like so many women during NPR's early days, she is tall. (Oddly, a number of the NPR men back then are pretty short.) I am bupkis—less than chopped liver.

As the seconds tick off on the countdown clock for the story that is currently playing, I try to explain to Susan how the intro should go. The information is all there, but the paragraphs need rearranging. I provided arrows. "Okay, Susan, you start here. Then go to the bottom paragraph, then back to the middle . . ."

:03 . . . :02 . . . :01

Susan's mic is opened. I shut up. She starts to read. Good, good. That's right. Then she stops. She's lost her place in the mess of arrows I've drawn on the script. Dead air, dead air, dead air. Then she figures out my chicken scratches, finishes reading the intro; her mic closes; the piece airs. The consummate pro.

I had had a similar situation with another host a few days before that.

His reaction: "If you can't make your fucking deadline, get someone in here who fucking can!"

Susan is exacting and a force of nature but also forgiving of a radio rookie. All she says is: "Honey, you need to get yourself a watch." It's the beginning of a beautiful friendship.

At first, I can only watch and learn as we sit in an edit booth listening to reel-to-reel tape, Susan smoking a cigarette and saying, "Yes, THAT'S the tape cut we need." She always knows her vision for a piece, but as time passes (and Susan quits smoking), she starts to trust my suggestions too. Sometimes, though, she'll say my idea for a transitional scene in a story is lame, and then I'll give her shit about the half-ass way she holds her microphone. She's one of the few people at NPR who calls me Pete.

Over the decades we have interviewed countless artists, authors and musicians, and worked together around the country and the world, from Kenya to Russia to Lithuania—all sorts of places. We even ended up living across the street from each other for many years, with Susan acting like an aunt to my twin daughters Eden and Danielle, looking on as they blossomed from babies into young women.

That script-crashing moment in the studio with Susan came at about week three or four of my NPR audition. And I almost didn't even make it that far.

I had decided to pursue a career at NPR after two years drifting around South America. Returning to the U.S., I was unemployed, with few marketable skills and no real notion of what I wanted to do with my life.

Unlike some of my future NPR colleagues, I wasn't a radiohead growing up—aside from listening to baseball games, The Beatles, storyteller Jean Shepherd, or the occasional heavyweight fight on my transistor radio under my pillow at bedtime.

My recording experience back then consisted of going over to my classmate Kenny Greenfield's house Saturday afternoons in seventh grade and cracking each other up taping absurd stories we ad-libbed into his father's Dictaphone. Years later I'd managed a degree in English and liked to write, but had never taken a journalism class. However, I had started listening to National Public Radio, and this seemed like something I might give a try. It would become my journalism grad school.

I had little to offer the place, so I figured I would write a gonzo cover letter (this was pre-email) highlighting my wandering in South America and the fact that I was an Eagle Scout. My inquiries to the network were answered with form letters from everyone except the executive producer of *ATC* at the time, Steven Reiner, who liked my travel and language experience (Spanish and Portuguese), as well as my saucy sense of humor.

He invited me down to D.C. to try out. This was a time when you could still sweet talk your way in the door at the organization. Today, they would have never let me out of the elevator. Our entry-level producers are scary smart and over-qualified. But in those years, NPR was small and fledgling and better suited for taking a risk on someone like me. I was terrified.

When I arrived in February, the city was frozen solid by an ice storm; and as this was the time of Mayor Marion Barry, whose approach to snowy streets was to tell residents to wait for spring, public transport was at a standstill. So I hitchhiked to the office.

When I got to the building, I discovered that Reiner was on vacation in Brazil, and he had not alerted anyone that I was coming. After some negotiating ("Who did you say you are?"), they cautiously let me inside.

My second day trying out an ice-encrusted Air Florida Flight 90 crashed during takeoff into the 14th Street Bridge and sank to the bottom of the frozen Potomac River, killing 78 people, 74 on board the plane and four on the bridge. Five people survived. The newsroom exploded. Editors, reporters and producers raced around making phone calls, writing copy, interviewing witnesses. It was an awful event but hugely intoxicating. As I tried to make myself useful, I knew then and there that this was what I wanted to do for a living.

As I've mentioned, I just barely made it through those initial days without getting tossed out with the recycling. (Actually, I don't think they even had recycling that far back.) At the time of my NPR audition, I had never edited audio tape, so I drenched myself in the process as intensely as I could. By the end of that first week, they decided to roll the dice and let me edit a simple phone interview.

I spent the entire day cutting this thing, amassing a tall stack of 10" silver aluminum reels in my edit booth full of outtakes—identical reels that I had neglected to label. I think you can see where this is headed.

As my deadline approached, I suddenly realized that I had completely lost track of which was the master reel with the body of the interview. With five minutes to air, the show producer poked his head into my edit booth.

"Everything okay?"

"Yup, just finishing up."

Well, I thought, I guess I'm not getting this job. But then for the first of what would become many times, the radio gods smiled upon me. I somehow fished the master reel out of the morass and handed it to the producer as he screamed into my edit booth with a minute to air. I have no idea what it sounded like, but the interview made it to broadcast and dead air was avoided.

On another day during my tryout time, I was standing in an editor's office waiting for an opportunity to pitch a story idea just as she was asking the reporter in front of me if he would be available that evening to cover a memorial service. It was for Oscar Romero, the El Salvadoran archbishop who had been assassinated while serving mass in San Salvador two years earlier.

The reporter said he couldn't. Then she turned to me, someone she had never met. "How about you? Can you cover this?" Not only had I never reported an NPR story before, but it would be a fairly quick turnaround for a neophyte—the next morning. Of course, I said, "Sure."

That night I followed the crowd that sang and chanted during their candlelight march through the streets and then recorded speakers in a downtown D.C. church as they eulogized Romero, recounting his activism and heroism in the face of right-wing death squads. Then I rushed back to NPR to start writing my piece.

It would have taken an experienced reporter a couple of hours to put this thing together. It took me all night. My five a.m. deadline seemed so far away when I started the process, but as the evening wore on, it came creeping closer and closer, like a tiger sniffing out prey.

People on the *Morning Edition* staff were very kind and helped me select my audio cuts (we call them *actualities* or *acts*) and coached me on my voicing. In the end, the piece made it to air; and I learned that when push came to shove, I could turnaround a story on deadline. It was a big confidence boost.

Despite my deadline fiascos, NPR was foolish enough to hire me. I kept filling in, and I think at some point people just assumed I had a job at the place, so they gave me an employee ID. To this day, I'm still waiting for an administrative person to discover some misplaced yellowed paperwork and come tell me, "You know what, you are not actually employed here, never have been."

And with the job came an instant love of making radio:

· It was creative. The rules were few as long as the story worked;
· It was cheap. You could do it with a simple tape recorder and microphone;
· It was low profile. You could work all by yourself; you didn't need the whole crew of people television required;
· It was intimate. You were whispering right into someone's ear;
· It was non-intrusive and didn't demand the listener's complete attention. They could drive to Poughkeepsie, make linguini with clam sauce or unclog the upstairs toilet while tuning in.

# Chapter 2

# We Happy Few

As I've said, National Public Radio was still a budding network in the 1980's. We were a tight-knit crew who knew each other well, unlike now when I regularly get into the elevator alongside three people with whom I've never had a conversation.

In my first days at the place, I found out that a grad student working part time on *ATC* played basketball. So one day AJ and I went out to shoot some hoops on a decrepit outdoor urban half-court at the Thaddeus Stevens Elementary School just a few blocks from the office.

Soon, other guys and a couple of women from work started joining us, then some more reporters, producers and editors, until we decided we should rent a gym. Thus was born the NPR Wednesday night pick-up basketball game—a ritual that continues to this day, some 40 years later.

Even though I'm really too old, I continue to show up most Wednesdays. Over the years, I've broken my nose, cracked my ribs and pulled too many muscles to count. My shooting percentage is approaching that of low-fat milk, and yet I keep at it because as one of our original members, one-time North Dakota all-state player and NPR economics correspondent John Ydstie put it, "Every now and then, I do something that feels like it felt when I was 20 years old. And you realize you were once really good at this thing. And I'm not very good at it anymore, but it's still fun."

The array of characters has transformed over the decades from almost exclusively NPR staffers to include journalists from other organizations as well as carpenters, doctors, locksmiths, IT guys, military guys, lawyers and at least one top White House staffer we kept hoping would surprise us one week by bringing along President Obama, who plays a pretty sweet game I'm told. That never happened.

Back in the day, on Thursday mornings NPR could look like an emergency room as we limped in with our pulled muscles, contusions and sprained ankles. Now the game is intergenerational. I'm older than the parents of some of the guys I play with. And when one of us graybeards goes down on the court, the young guys are quick to ask, "Are you okay? Are you okay?" and seem ready to dial 911. I guess that's when someone might say "at least he died doing what he loved."

There was a similar camaraderie amongst the rest of us early employees—*Nippers*, as we call ourselves. We were used to weathering periodic fiscal meltdowns and assaults from conservative members of Congress. As a matter of fact, soon after I was hired, I almost lost my job because of a financial crisis.

There had been some major money mismanagement and the network came close to going under in 1983. NPR President Frank Mankiewicz was forced to resign and the organization sagged under an almost $3-million-dollar budget deficit. To save the place, well over a hundred people were going to have to be let go.

As one of the last hired, I assumed I would be the first fired. I remember it was a Friday, and throughout the day people were being called into the news director's office one by one and given the ax. I sat fretting in my edit booth all day, cutting interviews and waiting for a cold tap on my shoulder.

At some point during the afternoon, the edit booth door swung open. It was the show producer telling me the news director wanted to see me. No wait, he's not saying that. He's merely checking the status of the interview I'm editing. I still had a job.

Despite the brush with obliteration, or maybe because of it, NPR employees felt a little bit renegade back then. Plus, we were not well known. When we'd call someone up for an interview, more often than not we'd have to explain who we were. "Kind of like the BBC for the

U.S." was the shorthand many of us used. Today a potential interview guest is much more likely to say, "Oh, I love you guys."

In addition to the rigorous straight-down-the-line reporters, the place was full of creative, smart ex-hippies and some not-so-ex who had come from innovative member stations and progressive media outlets. There was long hair, ridiculous mustaches, peasant dresses and parties most weekends, where it was not uncommon to be passing a joint to your boss. However, the journalism was fair, first rate and truthful, and the radio production values outstanding.

That building where I started on M Street south of Dupont Circle in Washington was NPR's second home, and we've moved twice more since then—always to bigger and more elegant digs. M Street was a warren of gray-cloth cubicles and snug little edit booths. Things went on behind those tightly shut doors besides tape editing. Rumor had it that more than one *Nipper* baby had been storyboarded in one.

There have been at least 80 NPR marriages (and now some divorces) over the decades. Susan Stamberg is keeper of the master list. My own wedding on Martha's Vineyard in 1997 to my wife Jessica Goldstein, an NPR producer at the time, had an NPR-heavy guest list. Jessica's parents owned a small house there that just happened to be down the same dirt road as the estate where then President Clinton and his family vacationed.

We knew they were going to be there when we got married; so we figured, what the heck, let's invite them to the wedding. But we heard nothing back.

Houses in that Vineyard neighborhood had access to a private beach people reached via outboard motor across a pond. On an overcast afternoon a couple of days before the wedding, Jessica and I had the sand to ourselves, except for a couple of Secret Service agents shuffling through the tick-infested shrubbery bordering the shoreline in their Bermuda shorts with calf-high black socks. And then a little putt-putt boat pulled up from the pond. Out stepped three people: Bill, Hillary and adolescent Chelsea.

The Clintons threw their blanket down about 30 yards from us. Just the presidential family, and Jessica and me, on that entire stretch of beach.

A little while later Bill and Hillary took a walk down the beach, passing right in front of us. In sweatshirts and shorts, hand in hand, they looked like any happy couple on a sandy stroll, although if my calculations about timing are correct, this was during the Monica Lewinsky liaison.

Everyone said hello and got to talking. We revealed where we worked, and the president said in that scratchy Arkansas lilt, "Oh, we love NPR". The politician who could light up a room could also brighten a cloudy day on the beach. We asked if they had gotten the wedding invite. They said no, but they wouldn't be able to make it anyway because they were all departing back to D.C. on the wedding day.

Then it was time for the photo op. As it was just the four of us (this was the pre-cell-phone-selfie epoch), Bill took a picture of Jessica and me with Hillary and then Hillary took a picture of us with Bill. It was a little awkward standing with the leader of the free world in our soggy bathing suits. Still, we framed those photos.

On the morning of our wedding, we put out white balloons along the dirt road leading to the house to guide our guests. I should also mention that the United States government "massaged" the president's scheduled departure time, moving it up a bit so that it didn't cause a traffic jam with people arriving for the wedding.

Just before the ceremony began a White House staffer delivered a lovely letter from the president and first lady congratulating us and wishing us the best. The next day I read an article in the *Boston Globe* detailing the president's exit from the Vineyard, noting the white balloons neighbors had strung along the road to wish him farewell.

NPR's Scott Simon nearly missed the ceremony when his flight to the Vineyard from Boston was delayed to clear airspace for the president's departure. This being Scott—who in some ways is a throwback to an earlier era of cultured formality—he was the only guy to show up in a blazer and tie even though we had said dress was casual. Ever since that day, he has ridiculed my wedding outfit of a cream colored vest and linen pants as something the weaker half of Sonny and Cher might have worn.

Susan Stamberg spent most of her time talking and laughing with my New Jersey childhood friends who regaled her with stories of our knuckleheaded past.

A few days later when Jessica and I were checking in for our honeymoon flight to Barcelona, I shamelessly pulled out the congratulatory correspondence from Bill and Hillary. I showed it to the gate agent and said something like, "I have a letter from the President of the United States requesting that you upgrade us to business class." She gave a sly smile and actually did put us in the fancy seats.

The NPR building where so many romances had begun was kind of a dump by the time we moved out—cigarette burns, broken chairs, a hole in the wall where an angry producer had frisbeed a metal tape reel. I still remember the day when a show editor told a reporter that her piece would not be airing. She got so angry that she flung her coffee mug against the wall, shattering it and leaving a brown dripping Jackson Pollack. That stain remained until the day we vacated.

Other stains were not the result of food fights, just the journalists' obsession with food. It seems like we will sloppily gorge ourselves on anything that isn't made of fiberglass, as though we've been on bread-and-water rations for months. Put out a spread on a table, and it's attacked like a swarm of locusts moving through a field of grain. Nothing remains in the aftermath but paper plates and olive pits, well, maybe not even the pits.

**Chapter 3**

# Ping-Pong With Commander Zero

Hearing our correspondents report on the civil wars in Central America in the early 1980's, I thought to myself, I want to do that kind of stuff.

To my astonishment, within the first few months of my hire, NPR gave me a chance to prove myself overseas. It wasn't just any foreign assignment; it was a presidential visit to South and Central America with Ronald Reagan. To this day, it remains the only time I have ever traveled with a U.S. president. I was greener than a sprig of cilantro.

I got to go because Reagan was headed first to Brazil and I was the only producer on staff who spoke some Portuguese. Paired with a veteran State Department correspondent, I was excited beyond belief, although I think he may have hoped for a more seasoned companion.

This was the big time. On the media plane I sat next to guys I usually watched on TV. As the press corps, we were treated differently. I mean, the flight attendants didn't even ask us to buckle our seat belts. I thought they might sit on our laps.

The highlight of this trip for me didn't happen while covering the American president and the demonstrations that greeted him in a few places. It came after we peeled off from the official entourage for a story in Costa Rica. Through an intermediary we had arranged to be taken to interview dissident Nicaraguan rebel leader Edén Pastora, often known by his nom de guerre, Commander Zero.

Pastora's claim to fame came during the revolution against the dictatorship of Anastasio Somoza in Nicaragua in the 1970's. He led an assault on the National Palace in Managua, taking hundreds of hos-

TRIP OF
PRESIDENT REAGAN
TO BRAZIL, COLOMBIA,
COSTA RICA AND HONDURAS
November 30-December 4, 1982

# WHITE HOUSE PRESS

PETER BRESLOW
NAME

NPR Radio Engineer
AFFILIATE

tages, many of them legislators and government officials, and using them as bargaining chips to free imprisoned Sandinista rebels, including leaders Daniel Ortega and Tomás Borge. He also managed to get the Somoza regime to pony up half a million dollars and a plane to Cuba.

But after the Sandinistas defeated Somoza, Pastora became disillusioned with the Ortega-led government and founded an insurgent group to work against them in the south, while the right-wing-rebel Contras, with major U.S. support, tried to overthrow them from the north. (Today Daniel Ortega is still in power and considered by many to be a corrupt authoritarian.)

On our visit to Costa Rica, the plan was to interview Pastora at his hideout high in the peaks outside of San Jose. One morning our contact picked us up for the windy drive into the mountains. I was hoping for a blindfold, but they decided to let us enjoy the scenery.

We arrived at a clearing with some simple housing. Lounging around and playing table tennis were guys in military garb. And then appeared a short man with a barrel chest who clearly garnered respect from all those around him. This was Commander Zero, hero of the Nicaraguan revolution. I thought about the attack he had led on the National Palace and the exultant photo I'd seen of him boarding the airplane to Cuba, dressed in fatigues, black beret, both arms raised in triumph, a rifle in one hand and two hand grenades pinned to bandoliers across his chest.

On this day, though, there were no grenades visible. Pastora was amiable and serious. I'm sure we had a profound discussion about the plight of Nicaragua, but what I mostly remember from that afternoon was his ping-pong game. It was pretty good, but I probably could have beaten him. For the sake of the revolution, however, I let *Comandante Cero*, who died in 2020, win.

In reality, the most hair-raising part of this assignment came as I was arriving home from the airport back in Washington. Once again D.C. was covered in an ice sheet, and my cab driver was very nervous driving. He told me he had been a law professor in Kabul and fled over the mountains on foot after the Russians invaded. Today he was worried about negotiating D.C.'s roadways.

As we came down a side street, we went into a skid. Through the windshield, I saw a guy with his back to us trying to push his car out of an icy patch. We were rolling silently towards him.

I desperately tried to roll down the taxi window and yell a warning, but before I knew it, we had slammed into his car. I thought for sure his legs had been crushed, but somehow he was not injured. My cab driver was so shaken he refused to get back behind the wheel. "You drive, you drive", he said. That's right; my very first NPR assignment ended with me driving my own cab home.

# Chapter 4

# Managua, Mugabe's Revenge, Smuggling Human Ashes

Not long after my table tennis tournament with Edén Pastora, NPR sent me to Nicaragua to work with reporter Tom Gjelten, who was covering the Contra conflict at the time. One story we reported was in the north of the country where earlier the Contras had blown up a vehicle, killing civilians. We decided to accompany a truck transporting people and traveling that same route some days later.

Tom, who is braver than I am, climbed into the open bed of the truck while our driver and I followed behind in a car. As we rolled along a rutted road, I sat in the front seat with my finger ready to release the pause button on my tape machine if an explosion rang out. Thank goodness, my finger remained in place. (Years later in Angola I did miss the explosion of an incoming rebel mortar at an airfield because I had stopped rolling just prior. I always felt bad about that.)

There was also a very wacky story we reported, about the visit by televangelist Jimmy Swaggart to the capital Managua. This was shortly before revelations of his cavorting with prostitutes led to his defrocking by the Assemblies of God. Swaggart was in all his glory as he orated in the brightly lit Plaza of the Revolution one night. Looking very much the cousin of early rock-and-roll bad boy Jerry Lee Lewis, Swaggart gesticulated, panted and preached in perfect synch with his equally animated interpreter.

A glassy-eyed crowd seemed transfixed as they stumbled towards the stage to drop whatever offerings they could into the collection buckets. I wonder if any of them got to watch the broadcast of Swaggarts's tearful confession for his sins, which came just a week later.

When I arrived in Managua the government had just frozen the currency. They were about to devalue it; but during the process you couldn't spend the current bills. As Nicaragua was a place where credit cards didn't function at the time, this basically meant that everything was closed—hotels, restaurants, supermarkets—all shuttered for about three days.

But a population that had lived under the pilfering regime of dictator Anastasio Somoza learns to make do. With no functioning restaurants, enterprising housewives set up makeshift to-go stands out their kitchen windows, which is how we dined and how I likely contracted hepatitis A.

About a month after returning from that assignment, I gradually started feeling weaker and weaker. In the end, I couldn't lift myself off the couch. It remains a bit of a mystery that I contracted the illness in the first place, as I was diagnosed with hep A years before in Brazil, and you're supposed to be immune for life once you've had it.

Considering some of the places I've been sent on assignment, I've remained remarkably healthy, a lot of it due to diligence. One time traveling into the Amazon to report on deforestation, correspondent David Welna and I were stopped at a government health outpost. Before we could proceed, they required a yellow fever inoculation, which we didn't have.

The worker at the checkpoint, not a health care professional I can assure you, offered to give us shots. He stuck David first, wiped off the needle and then tried to stick me. Now David is a friend with, I'm sure, some of the purest blood flowing in anyone's veins, but I insisted on a new needle nonetheless.

One technique I developed over the years for circumventing Montezuma's or Mohammed's or Mugabe's revenge is to chew two Pepto Bismol tablets every morning when I'm in a region where I might encounter some questionable edibles. Sure, you are left sporting chalky pink lips, but you also give your stomach just the slightest edge for fighting off something funky.

There is another assignment from those first years that I still cherish more than most of the others. Vietnam. I traveled there with writer Nguyen Qui Duc, who was returning for the first time since he fled as a teenager when the North Vietnamese entered Saigon in 1975.

His father, a high provincial official, had been captured at gunpoint in the city of Hue during the 1968 Tet offensive, as 9-year-old Duc looked on, and was held prisoner for years.

Eventually, the entire family did make it out and to the U.S., except for Duc's mentally-ill sister, who died in country. One of the reasons for our trip was to retrieve her ashes. Duc later wrote a book about the experience called, *Where the Ashes Are*.

Americans were few and far between on the streets of Ho Chi Minh City and Hanoi back then and when we were spotted with our microphones, jubilant crowds would gather just to touch us.

We collected Duc's sister's ashes from a Buddhist temple, a profoundly moving moment as Duc tearfully chanted while a monk's bell chimed, the excited crowd outside the temple squealed, and a pounding cloudburst doused everything. The audio was thrilling.

Now the question was how to get the ashes out of the country without jumping through the Communist bureaucratic hoops we were certain awaited us. We would smuggle them, of course. So we transferred the remains from the urn that held them into a small cardboard box. All seemed good until the day before we were scheduled to depart, when Duc was contacted by the authorities and told to come into headquarters.

We were nervous. This was the 1980's, Vietnam was just starting to open up, and the government was still hardcore Communist. We had been assigned an official minder to keep track of our reporting (people we interviewed were later questioned by the police) and we didn't know what to expect. I paced in my hotel room.

An hour or so later Duc returned sweating, but smiling. It seems the police had found the empty urn where we'd left it in our hotel room in another city days before and were just wondering if we wanted it back. Whew!

Those ashes made it across the border into Thailand, then to the U.S. and, ultimately, to a place of prominence in Duc's family home in San Francisco. I am sad to say my friend Duc died in 2023.

# Chapter 5

# Pilottown

Some of my greatest audio collaborations have been with one of NPR's greatest reporters and storytellers, Austin based John Burnett. We have traveled the world together bonding over the blues, bicycling and bourbon.

One of our first trips occurs on a bright spring week in 1991 down near the mouth of Mississippi to report on river pilots. These are local watermen who hop aboard the giant tankers coming in from the sea headed up north to New Orleans. They know the idiosyncrasies of the river's tides and currents, where the shallows are, and can be trusted to navigate the huge vessels safely into port.

When they are on duty, the pilots live in a little village constructed on piers in the marshes called Pilottown, located in Plaquemines Parish about 85 miles south of New Orleans. The place is built on stilts just a few feet above the river, so a string of walkways connects everything. As you might imagine, Pilottown sustained heavy damage during Hurricane Katrina. However, we are there well before then, and the place is bustling.

A longtime resident shows us around telling us about the fauna. "It's all variety of boids . . . red boids, blue boids, yellow boids." With John, you can count on finding good accents and exceptional tape for your stories. I've always been envious of his getting to live in Texas, where it seems everyone is a natural storyteller with just the right twang in their voice to keep things lively.

After our wildlife tour, I wander into the living quarters, where a television is turned to CNN. I walk up to the TV to record a bit of sound in case we want to use it in the story when I notice on the screen a shot of the No. 42 bus I take to work every morning in Washington. It's on fire.

There are riots in my neighborhood, the ethnically diverse Mt. Pleasant section of the city. Some residents, upset about the shooting of a Salvadoran man by the police, spend a couple of days fighting with the cops, looting and setting vehicles on fire. I anxiously call NPR and ask if they can send someone up to my house to make sure it's still standing. A few hours later I get the all clear.

John and I have plans to accompany one of the pilots once a ship approaches Pilottown. In the wee hours of the morning, we get the word. The Ariel, a Norwegian-flagged tanker carrying 55-thousand tons of heavy fuel oil from Amsterdam, is close. Now these giant vessels don't just pull over and wait for you to board; you've got to leap onto them as they head upstream.

We approach alongside the 800-foot-long chugging ship in a little launch as the crew above throws down a flexible ladder for us to ascend. The steep gray side of the tanker seems to stretch up to the heavens and I wonder how I am going to negotiate the climb all the while holding a microphone and tape machine, not to mention making sure my recording levels are right.

I also question how the pilot we are tagging along with, Adolph Ajubita, a guy who looks like he really enjoys his jambalaya, is going to spring from our tiny boat and make it up that ladder. But the man is a marvel. Incredibly light on his feet, he dances his way up the ladder like a gymnast. John and I are a bit less graceful, but we manage to board the ship and sail all the way up to New Orleans. Many more escapades with John are to follow over the years.

# Chapter 6

# Breslow's Luncheonette

Despite living a mere eight miles from Manhattan, I came from a place where neighborhood kids trapped and skinned muskrats down at the creek and sold the pelts. Little Daniel Boons and Jerimiah Johnsons in the shadow of the Empire State Building.

Every summer I spent two weeks at Camp NoBeBoSco, a Boy Scout camp in northwest Jersey. There, I worked on the merit badges that ultimately earned me the rank of Eagle Scout.

My troop, Troop 85, was kind of the *F Troop* of Bergen County, screw ups who got lost on hikes and had to be rescued. We once ended up camping behind a shopping mall just off the highway where headlights shined through our tent flaps as we tried to sleep.

One winter we had a Klondike Derby, for which we built an Idi-tarod-type sled minus the Huskies. But there was no snow that season so we dragged our sleds on the road, sparks flying.

Another year an unseemly episode unfolded during a Morse code competition. One scout was given a message in dots and dashes on an index card to transmit via semaphore flags to another troop member at the other end of a gymnasium. But the first scout inadvertently held the card upside down so the message he sent was complete gibberish. When the receiving scout realized what his troopmate had done, he reared back and belted him in the jaw. Several basic tenants of the Scout Law were shattered with that punch, and we were banished.

In my earlier Scouting years, the real joy at Camp NoBeBoSco came not from making fires with flint and steel or learning how to tie a bow-

Getting ready for my Eagle Scout award ceremony with my dad.

line or sheepshank. It was the summertime sex talks conducted by our troop leader, Lenny Hacker, which made Troop 85's campsite one of the most popular.

A couple of nights a week after taps, the horny kids from the Catholic troops (we were mostly the Jewish scouts) would sneak out of their bunks to come to our area to listen to Lenny rave on about his sexual conquests and give masturbation 101 instructions. Today, I'm sure Lenny would be locked up, but back then you could get away with things.

Central to my New Jersey upbringing was *Breslow's Luncheonette*.

*Breslow's* was a neighborhood candy store my father owned in Hackensack. It was his father's before that. For more than 50 years, *M. Breslow's and Sons*—the *Sons* meant my dad and his brother Irv—

stood at the top of the hill on Essex Street with its comic books, toys and a lunch counter sporting decades of gum stuck underneath.

At lunchtime, the swivel counter stools—with maroon padding— would be filled with doctors, nurses and orderlies from the Hackensack Hospital just down the street. They ordered cheeseburgers and Western omelets, lime rickeys and vanilla milkshakes.

My father began working in the store when he was a teenager and later on had plans to study dentistry, but the Depression interfered. After World War II, during which he was a flight instructor for the Navy, he hoped to become a commercial pilot. Unluckily for him, the airlines had their pick of accomplished post-war pilots, and my dad was slightly older than they preferred. A bit later he and a friend looked into opening a flight school in New Hampshire, but my mother refused to leave her family back in New Jersey.

When my grandfather became ill, my father got pulled back into *Breslow's* to help out, and never left. His became a life unfulfilled. In later years, my father would get his excitement vicariously, pulling out maps to follow my international adventures for NPR.

When I was very young, the place had a jukebox and a pinball machine, but they attracted "hoodie"—short for hoodlum—kids from Hackensack High, so one day my father removed them. The pinball ended up in our basement, where it developed an electrical short, and you had to be prepared for a shock every so often when you hit the flippers.

I started working at the store when I was about 11, getting up in the dark at 5 a.m. on Sundays to go in with my father to assemble and stack the newspapers—the *Daily News*, the *Newark Star-Ledger*, the *Bergen Record* and the *New York Times*. Around Christmas, the *Times* seemed thicker than the combined volumes of our *World Book Encyclopedia*.

After a few years of this, I was replaced by a neighborhood kid named Tubby, and I graduated to become a weekend soda jerk. I could make a mean BLT and chocolate egg cream, but I had a very difficult time flipping fried eggs on the grill without breaking the yolks.

From behind the counter, I gained perspective on how Dave Breslow made *Breslow's* work. Between orders, I would watch him at the cash register, selling the mailman some razor blades he'd never intended to buy ("What's-a-matter, you didn't have time to shave this morning?") or inveigle the doctor to have an after-lunch smoke ("Hey Doc, how about a good cheap cigar?).

All the while, my Yiddish-accented Russian-born grandmother would be calling her son on the phone from the apartment above the store, convinced that Ann, the sweet waitress who worked for years at *Breslow's*, was stealing the quarters my dad let pile up on the lip of the cash register. "Dave, she's robbin' you blind!"

This same grandmother, responding to my sister's question about when a framed photograph of my late grandfather had been taken replied, "Vhen he vas alive." And to me she would often say, "You never come see me, Peteky. Come see me and I'll give you all my money when I die."

As his fingers flew over the register keys, Dave maintained a rolling banter with everyone, keeping the wisecracks flying; and the locals kept coming back. I think they secretly liked being nudged into those extra razor blades; it made them feel a part of something—the neighborhood, maybe. And my dad was at his happiest at that busy spot behind the register with the customers, much happier really, than he ever seemed at home.

Dave spent his life in that store. At home, he would always complain about how "bushed" he was from working so hard, but he never returned to our house early from the place to spend more time with his wife and three kids. So I contented myself to see my father when we were both at work on the weekends.

*Breslow's* was never a gold mine, modestly supporting two families— my uncle's and ours—but in the early 1970's things turned bleak. *Toys R Us* was selling model airplane kits cheaper retail than my father could get them wholesale and *7-Eleven* was offering Big Gulps to go to people who no longer had the time to sit down for a lime rickey.

My father with the Phillies King Cheroot Cowgirl,
Hackensack, New Jersey, c. 1962

As good as he was behind the counter, my father was no match for the chain operations.

None of his children could help either. There was never any question of my taking over the store. My mother's standard line when anyone asked about the possibility of her only son carrying on the luncheonette tradition was, "I'll chop his legs off first," which makes it very tough working behind the counter.

In the end, my dad sold the luncheonette. For all his bellyaching about the store, he seemed lost once he got rid of the place. He had too much time on his hands. He stopped going out, and often stayed in his pajamas all day. Suddenly, he looked old and tiny.

Then the luncheonette itself disappeared. The Hackensack Hospital turned into the massive Hackensack University Medical Center and what was left of *Breslow's* was gobbled up, knocked down and turned into the hospital parking garage. Years later, when I visited my father as he lay dying in the hospital, I used to park my car in that garage, the site of the place that for more than 50 years bore his name.

A little bit of *M. Breslow's and Sons* does survive, however. On a wall in our den is the rectangular sign that used to hang out front on Essex Street. It is large, white and plastic, and above the red Coca-Cola logo are big black letters saying, BRESLOW'S LUNCHEONETTE.

On the adjacent wall is a promotional photo taken in the store. My father is in front of the cash register with displays of pocket combs and pens just behind him.

Beside him stands a very pretty model dressed up like a cowgirl, advertising Phillies King Cheroot cigars. My dad has one arm around the cowgirl, a Cheroot in his other hand and a mischievous grin on his face as he eyes the model. At that moment Dave Breslow looks like he could sell a pack of Phillies—a good cheap cigar—to just about anyone.

# Chapter 7

# Harebrained Jersey

The stage was set for an adventurous life in storytelling growing up in New Jersey. There I was surrounded by a coterie of friends, with whom I'm still tight more than 50 years later. We had hijinks and close calls, lots of them.

Many of our mishaps centered around our automobiles. In high school, my friend Lefty Monahan owned a convertible MG Midget, but that car was so small and Lefty was so tall that when the top was down, he would drive looking OVER the windshield. When the top was up, he had to crank his head to the side to fit.

One drunken evening, with our friend John passed out on the lawn, that Midget somehow got pushed up onto the grass and rolled silently, inexorably towards him. At the last possible moment, Lefty—who was now trotting alongside the convertible, leaning over and steering from OUTSIDE the car—saw John and screamed. John rolled to the side with nothing more serious than grass stains.

On another night, a pack of about 10 of us thought it would be fun to go out in the street in front of the high school and fake beating up Lefty as cars drove by. Of course, the first car that passed was a cop who slammed on his brakes, jumped out and gave chase screaming "Halt! Halt!" We scattered through the neighborhood wondering if he was going to shoot. Some people got caught, but I hid out in a friend's basement until the coast was clear.

Back then I chose my footwear based on whether I thought there might be a chance of getting pursued. Sneakers were good, sandals were bad. I might have been wearing sneakers one Cabbage Night in junior high school, but they didn't help.

Cabbage Night was what we called the night before Halloween when we would go out and mess things up: rub soap on car windshields, squirt shaving cream at each other, heave rolls of toilet paper across shrubs and trees and toss eggs at moving cars.

On this night I picked the wrong car to egg. Inside were two tough-looking greasers and their girlfriends. One guy leaped out and sprinted after me. I took off, hoping to make it to the safety of my own house. With the leaves off the trees, I could see our kitchen lights shining in the distance as I hightailed it through the suburban backyards, chest heaving. I didn't make it.

The guy tackled me and then punched my lights out. Stumbling, he dragged me back to his car where I remember seeing the girlfriends in the backseat smirking. I was doomed. But just as he was about to shove me in and slit my throat, a police car came around the corner and the young hoodlums took off, leaving me at the curb. This time I was saved by the cops.

Most of our cars back then had names: Ernst, Rocky, Duke, Fred, Walter, Dorf, Ignatz and Slum Bum.

Ernst was my father's 1958 Chevy Biscayne that I inherited. At some point, one of my friends found a spare key to it I'd dropped, so periodically I would walk out of the house and Ernst wouldn't be there in front where I had parked it, but rather sitting in a neighbor's driveway down the street. This went on for the better part of a year before my friend finally fessed up when he saw I was about to lose my mind.

Ernst's floor eventually got so rusted out that one night as I was cruising around (I'm pretty sure we were joyriding through a cemetery) the driver's seat partially collapsed through the floorboard, and I could no longer see over the steering wheel. I had to squat on the seat to get Ernst home.

Rocky was our ruby red 1962 Ford Falcon. My close call with this car happened when it caught on fire as I was pulling up to the pump at a gas station, flames spewing from under the chassis. The station attendant rightfully freaked out and started screaming to get the car away from all that gasoline. But when I tried to drive off, I found the rear wheels had seized from the heat. The station guy flew over in his tow truck and skidded Rocky and me to safety.

On a freezing cold night a couple of years later, I was driving Fred, a 1964 Chevy Bel Air, on the interstate in Connecticut with a backpack full of weed beside me when the car sputtered to a halt. I opened the hood; the engine was glowing red. Fred suffered from an undiagnosed oil leak.

Quickly, a Connecticut state trooper pulled up behind us and before I knew it, I was sitting in the backseat of his squad car with several ounces of pot in my lap, which in those days could lead to some serious jail time. Fortunately, the cop just called for a tow truck and drove us to the bus station.

We were pretty bored boys who didn't have much success with the girls, but our cars helped break the tedium. We used them when we appropriated laughing gas stored on the loading dock behind the local hospital. Using a wrench, we'd crank open the spigot on the tank of nitrous oxide, put our mouths on the nozzle and inhale deeply. Ah—a few moments in Never Never Land.

And when there was a snow day in high school we slid in our boots along the empty snow packed Garden State Parkway hanging onto the open car doors like we were water skiing.

Later on, there were other cars, including a couple of late 1960's era Volvos (one I called Mona, the other remained nameless) and each came fully equipped with a near miss or two.

I drove Mona when I was attending college in western Massachusetts and living in a dilapidated wood-heated farmhouse with a quirky group of musicians, potters, banjo makers, three goats who hung out on our porch and mushrooms popping up through the damp floor in the bathroom. We raised rabbits, made our own bread and had a huge garden surrounded by an electrified fence to keep out the cows that grazed nearby. I regularly got zapped when I would crawl under it through the wet morning grass, rather than walk all the way around to the gate on the far side.

When I bought Mona, it had close to 200,000 miles on it and was trouble from day one. I was always working on it. One time after I had finally fixed the brakes, I excitedly took it for a test drive. But in my euphoria, I had neglected to tighten the lug nuts on one of the wheels. All of a sudden, as I was about to get on the highway, the car lurched to the right. I looked in the mirror and saw the rear passenger's side tire bounding into the woods. The Volvo sat tilted in the middle of the road while I went hunting for the wheel.

Late on another night, I was tooling home to the farmhouse after hearing my musical hero Muddy Waters perform, a young lady in the passenger seat. Up ahead I saw what appeared to be a truck making a left turn, so I passed on the right. But it was a FIRE truck (without its lights blinking I will add in my defense). And it wasn't making a left turn; it was swinging wide for a RIGHT turn.

The truck hit me square in the driver's door, sent the Volvo up on the curb, just missing a telephone pole. We all emerged unscathed; and with a non-matching color door replaced from a junkyard, I continued to drive that car.

I was driving my other nameless Volvo headed back to New Jersey when my friend David jumped out of the car at about 1 a.m. on the George Washington Bridge. We had gone to a Yankee game in the Bronx and gotten hammered on cheap beer. After the game, we stumbled around on the street with no idea where we'd parked the car. At last, we spotted it and I started driving home, with David lying down in the back seat.

All of a sudden on the bridge, he sat up, remembered he lived in lower Manhattan, not Jersey, opened the car door and was gone.

The close calls didn't let up. One weekend a group of us were camping in upstate New York. We ended up taking some mescaline and headed into town to a redneck bar called Big Jane's. There at the end of the bar sat Jane, in all her bigness. In our hallucinogenic haze, we were not the most well-behaved long hairs at the pool table. Pretty soon, the locals had had enough and booted us into the parking lot, where a pummeling was surely waiting.

Somehow, we got out of there unscathed, but we worried they would follow us back to our campsite and finish the job, kind of like what happened to Jack Nicholson's character in the movie *Easy Rider*, which had just come out. It was an uneasy—but thankfully uneventful—night in the tent.

On another outdoors trip, we ended up at a gorge with a sheer 30-foot cliff that dropped into a deep pool. I had gotten into cliff diving a year or two earlier, and this day I thought I would climb up and give this one a go. However, when I got to the ledge and peered down, I realized that in the intervening months, my bravado had waned. I was scared shitless.

With a crowd of people below gazing up in anticipation, there was no way I could climb down. So I jumped. But in some kind of reflex reaction, I grabbed for an overhanging branch, which flipped me over backwards and straight down the wall, instead of soaring out beyond it. I could actually hear the crowd gasp as I awkwardly plummeted. Again, luck was with me and I just cleared the rocks at the bottom. That was my last cliff dive.

I am so glad to have had daughters instead of sons. They seem much less likely to try this crazy ass stuff. But maybe I'm just kidding myself.

# Chapter 8

# Joe Schleppitone

That night on the George Washington Bridge with my friend David might have been the last Yankee game I ever attended. But as a kid, the Yankees were very much a part of my life; a number of the players lived in my New Jersey town, which was just a half-hour drive from the stadium.

One morning when I went to shortstop Tony Kubek's house to get his autograph, his wife said he was sleeping. Still, the ballplayer stumbled to the door in his bathrobe to sign my glove. Can you imagine that happening today with a pro athlete at his mansion?

Not all the Yankees were nice. When I was 12 or 13, my father took me to a game. Afterwards, I waited on the sidewalk outside the players' entrance hoping to grab another autograph or two. But the shining stars of baseball, men whose photographs were plastered on my bedroom wall, just blew past me.

Then first baseman Joe Pepitone came out the door making a beeline for his big white car, maybe a Cadillac, parked on the street. Joe was one of the first players to use a hairdryer in the clubhouse, perhaps that's why my Uncle George called him Schleppitone. I trailed alongside him as he walked down the sidewalk begging, "Come on Joe . . . sign my mitt . . .please!"

After he got in his car I shoved my glove through the open window, "Please Joe?" To this the ballplayer replied, "Get your arm out of my car, kid." Then he hit the button and put the window up on me. I yanked my arm back just in time. Years down the road I shed few tears when I heard that Schleppitone had gotten busted and was going to serve time for drug possession.

Even Hall of Fame Yankee broadcaster Red Barber, the Ol' Red Head as he was known, brushed me off that day. This was the same Red Barber who decades later would charm *Morning Edition* listeners with his weekly conversations with host Bob Edwards about baseball's bygone days and the camellias he cultivated in retirement in Florida. I came to resent those damn flowers.

# Chapter 9

# Audio 101

I started out in radio during the pre-digital age, when we edited sound by physically cutting ¼-inch tape with a single-edged razor blade. In the years that followed, I would become one of the fastest cutters in the company.

I became adept at quickly trimming a 35-minute interview into four succinct minutes on the radio, distilling the essence of what someone had said, kind of like a photographer capturing the character of a scene with a single photo.

With this new skill came an audio lingo glossary: acts, trax, ambi, tape cut, crossfade, fade up, fade down, butt cut, tease tape, vox, water-fall, gain, post, hit hot, two-way, three-way, stand up, SOC out, mix-down, backtime, deadroll, top and tail, in the clear, tape synch, phoner, Comrex, ISDN, apparent levels, intro, back announce, up cut, split track, sum to mono, mult-box, outtake and, of course, room tone.

I found a certain tactile pleasure in editing tape. There was a rhythm: mark the edit points with a white grease pencil; put the pencil in my mouth; put the tape in the edit block; make the cut with the razor blade; fasten it with splicing tape. Repeat, over and over again.

Occasionally, things would go wrong while cutting an interview— likely the only copy of the tape that existed. Sometimes it would get caught and wind around one of the spools on the editing deck. Then you had to gently uncoil it and try to flatten out the wrinkles so the interviewee didn't sound like they were warbling. When the tape was unsalvageable, you would just have to lose that part of the interview. Now, of course, the digital master file is always there to fall back on.

My cutting became instinctual and as I gained experience, I could listen to the tape at double speed and get lost in the editing process for hours, kind of like how I'd previously been absorbed in the darkroom when working on my photography. It was meditative.

There came a point where I could just tell by the rhythm of the interviewee's speaking when something they were saying was parenthetical and, therefore, expendable. It seems odd, but I almost didn't need to understand the content. I could just tell by the sound and the cadence.

Some tape cutters would create transcripts of the conversations to figure what to keep and what to shed. Others listened to the interviews (we call them two-ways) over and over again. Not me.

Usually, I knew the first time I listened through what to keep. As a matter of fact, if I heard the tape too many times, I became inured to it, and my decision-making turned muddled. After all, I figured the audience only got to hear the interview once, so what jumped out at me on first listen was likely to be what would stick in their minds as well.

I recall working with a reporter in Jerusalem during a series we were producing about the 50th anniversary of Israeli statehood. In his office smoking a cigarette with his feet up on a desk, he listened over and over again to possible tape cuts for his piece that he had put on a continuous loop. I couldn't bear it.

In the old days, many producers saved their outtakes either on a separate reel or taped up to the edit booth wall, dangling like long strands of brown audio fettuccine. It may sound arrogant, but most of the time I didn't retain my outtakes at all because I was confident in my decisions, although my editing habits did drive a few show producers a bit nuts.

In the end, of the countless interviews I've edited over the decades, not a single interviewee has ever complained about being misrepresented. Who would? We remove ums, ahs and stammers and make everyone sound more cogent than they've ever been in their lives.

This scrupulousness is not confined just to the editing of interviews. Audio can be a deceitful medium if you are inclined that way. Without pictures, who is ever going to know that the car-driving sound you are playing underneath your narration really wasn't recorded while you were driving back from that farm in Alabama you just reported on?

What if you forgot to roll tape during that drive? Why not just use some driving sound (ambi is what we call it, short for ambiance) you recorded last year on a trip to Iowa? Because it's not ethical. You could be headed down a slippery slope, where you start faking things that really matter. And now with AI anything is possible. But we cannot betray the listeners' trust that we will be scrupulously honest.

At the same time, it is that very lack of pictures that unleashes the audio storyteller's secret weapon: our listeners' imagination. When it's prodded by vivid sound and some crisp writing, it can often conjure up an image much more evocative than that of a television camera.

I once reported a piece about the implosion of an old high-rise public housing project in Kansas City. National Geographic television was there doing the same story about the three buildings simultaneously coming down. In the end, I believe our depiction of the collapsing structures—goosed by chest-vibrating explosion audio—was much more resonant than the visual story.

# Chapter 10

# Sound Judgment

For years, recording technicians were the guardians of the audio quality of what we put on the air. They went out in the field with me, sometimes recording in impeccable stereo. Having a talented engineer with you was like having an extra producer, a second set of ears searching for audio elements to make a story come alive. With them doing the recording, the producer could concentrate full-time on the storytelling. As they say, radio is a team sport.

Like all of us, engineers could be a temperamental gang, and you wanted to keep on their good side. I'm afraid I crossed that line one time in the Rockies. I was working with reporter John Burnett and a scientist on a story tracing the Rio Grande River. We were traveling in a minivan climbing a pass in the San Juan Mountains of southwestern Colorado to find a glacier whose summertime melting helped feed the headwaters of the Rio Grande.

Our deadline that day was tight because we were unsure if the top of the pass was clear of snow, which would allow us to drop into the town of Silverton. If not, and we got up there after dark, it would be a hairy return trip back down on the rocky road we'd come up.

We had a renowned sound technician with us, one of NPR's finest, but she could sometimes be a tad unforgiving. In her defense, I will say that the recording for this story had to be perfectly pristine stereo because it was for *Radio Expeditions*, NPR's collaboration with the National Geographic Society, whose hallmark was absolutely immaculate sound.

*Radio Expeditions* stories were some of the greatest gigs of all time (and where I met my wife, who was a producer with the program). It was exciting for me to team up with National Geographic, a place I had dreamed of working at as a kid. (I once even wrote them a letter asking what I should study in college to get hired at the magazine. I still can't believe it, but an editor wrote me back!)

Aside from traveling long swaths of the Rio Grande, I took part in other adventures as part of the *Radio Expeditions* team. I got to hang out with Tarahumara Indians in the Sierra Madre mountains of Mexico as they gathered to celebrate Easter Week by swilling some truly awful homemade corn beer called tesguino and dancing themselves delirious. I also profiled adventurer Will Steger in the Boundary Waters of Minnesota as he trained for a polar expedition. And there was the search for tigers from the back of an elephant in the lowlands of Nepal (more on that later).

On the day we set out for the glacier, our tech had been a hundred yards or so below us for quite some time recording the drip, drip, drip of the glacier. But the sun was starting to dip, dip, dip, and we had to get going. Surely she had gotten all she needed. I knew there would be hell to pay, but I let loose with one of my ear-splitting two-fingered whistles.

As she trudged back up the ravine, I could just about hear the theme from *Jaws* pounding in my head. Standing by the van, John and I had an idea of what was coming. Our very nice scientist did not. "Peter," she said simply, "Why don't you go fuck yourself?" It was a very quiet ride over the pass, which, by the way, was clear of snow.

John and I were with a different NPR tech when we got into a scrape in Louisiana. We almost ended up on the wrong side of the prison bars covering a story at the state's infamous penitentiary, Angola.

I've reported stories in several prisons—from a program to help inmates positively channel their anger at San Quentin State Prison in California to a writing course called *How to Laugh at a Life Sentence* (taught by filmmaker John Waters) at the Jessup Correctional Institution in Maryland. Interviewing people who have been sentenced for unspeakable crimes can certainly be disconcerting, but Angola was a whole nother kettle of convicts.

The prison is located on a beautiful site along a bend in the Mississippi that was once a plantation populated by enslaved people from that southern African country. If you are fortunate enough to be a trustee at the prison, you might spend your days on horseback roaming the lush rolling fields. However, that's for the precious few. Angola is a maximum-security prison with a troubling and violent past. More than one person told us that if you are sentenced to life at Angola, you should plan on dying there. There's no getting out.

Our story was about an annual highlight for the prisoners, the Angola Prison Rodeo. Every year thousands of visitors flock to the penitentiary to watch these amateur cowpokes try their hand at roping, bull riding and convict poker, a favorite with the crowd, in which four felonious cowboys sit down for a card game in the middle of the arena. An ornery bull is then set on them. The last man to hold his seat is the winner.

It's an exciting, sometimes brutal day for convicted murderers, rapists and robbers who often have little else to look forward to in their lives at Angola. These men speak with pride about the competition and the bragging rights that come with a good performance.

We spend the afternoon interviewing visitors, participants and prisoner vendors who sell their crafts including miniature ball-and-chain keychains. Using wireless microphones, we record the oomphs and thuds as the cowboys are launched and land in the dust off the backs of bucking broncos.

We come back the next day for more interviews including one with warden Burl Cain. He is an imposing guy who impresses us with his compassionate talk about the men he is charged with looking after. We get a solid interview from him, but then as we are wrapping up, things turn very bad, very quickly.

As part of our reporting for this story we interviewed journalist Daniel Bergner, who wrote a book called *God of the Rodeo*, which was critical of the brutality of the event and what Bergner considered the exploitation of the prisoners. The author also took on Burl Cain, who he accused of abuse of power and financial improprieties.

We let slip that we had talked to Bergner; and with that, the warden becomes furious and demands we give him the tape of his just completed interview.

We say, no. Once you grant us an interview it's ours. That's when Cain brings in his security chief, who stands by the door with his arms folded. They want that interview, and they are not going to let us leave with it. And not only that, Cain insists we hand over all the tapes of the rodeo and the prisoners we recorded, which at that moment are sitting in our rental car in the prison parking lot. I fib and tell him they are back at our hotel.

John and I are both pretty panicked wondering what to do, but the person who is really squirming is the young sound technician who is traveling with us, Neil Tevault. This is his first road gig ever—yes, his first radio rodeo—and all of a sudden he is under house arrest. But all the while he is also thinking on his feet.

We are recording in a short-lived format called DAT, digital audio tape, which is basically a kind of small cassette. Neil knows that the prison has no way to playback in this obscure medium and check its content, so he is trying to subtly eject the recorded interview from his machine and replace it with a blank cassette that we would then hand over to the authorities.

Meanwhile, John and I are huddling on the phone in Cain's office bathroom with NPR legal. Our lawyer assures us that, yes, we are correct; once the warden agreed to the interview, it is legally ours. She gets on the phone with Cain and tells him that if he confiscates the tape, it will end badly for him. NPR will not let this slide. We will make certain that all the major news organizations find out about his attempts to stifle a free press.

Disgusted, Cain throws up his burly arms and tells us to get out, adding that NPR will never again be allowed into Angola. Over time, though, the warden simmered down; since then, other NPR reporters have been welcomed into Angola—and been allowed to leave. I should also mention that Cain's shady business dealings finally caught up with him, and he was forced to retire.

When you returned from assignment, the techs were your partners in the studio elegantly mixing the elements for your piece. During production, with reels of tape spinning on three or four machines at once— each containing a different element of the story you were producing (ambiance, interview tape cuts, voice tracks)—you could sometimes feel like an orchestra conductor instructing the engineer which machine to hit when, how to bring in a fade up of sound and when to fade it out. If you made a mistake, even a little one, you often had to backup and redo an entire portion of the mix.

Today many of those techs are gone, lost to budget cuts and improved technology that allows me to record decent audio myself and mix it on my own on the computer rather than collaboratively in the studio. The mixing part now takes longer and doesn't sound nearly as good to demanding ears; that's the nature of the business these days. However, engineers do still fill valuable roles, like enhancing the quality of our audio before it airs, solving all sorts of technical problems, and running the sound board in the studio during broadcasts.

# Chapter 11

# Experiencing Technical Difficulties

In 1997 in the city of Ponce on the southern coast of Puerto Rico, Scott Simon and I were interviewing Sister Isolina Ferré, an 80-year-old nun who was known as the Mother Theresa of the territory. She told poignant stories in such incredible detail that I found myself wondering how in the world I would ever be able to edit down the interview. Not to worry.

It turned out that the engineer traveling with us who was recording the session had left her machine in pause mode for the first 20 or so minutes of the interview. Once she realized her mistake, she quite matter-of-factly announced that we would have to start over again. We did; but, of course, the redo wasn't nearly as good, especially with an elderly interviewee.

As someone who is constantly screwing up, I am very forgiving when errors happen; in this situation, though, I just couldn't understand how she could make such an egregious mistake. When I am taping, I obsessively check my machine to make sure that my recording levels are in the proper range and that the numbers on the digital counter are constantly going up, rather than staying put, as they do when you are in pause mode. Had she, a trained professional, really not glanced at her tape recorder over the course of almost half an hour?

On another occasion, John Burnett and I were in Big Bend National Park in southwest Texas recording an expansive travelog with an audio engineer. For our story I was determined to capture the snort of a javelina, the little wild animals with nasty tusks that roam the region.

After tromping up and down through hot dusty arroyos half the day, we spotted one just sitting out in the open on the lawn of one of the park employee's houses. I said, "Let's go after it." But by this point, the engineer had had enough of schlepping around her huge and heavy Nagra reel-to-reel recording device (which jurisdictionally I was prohibited from operating according to the engineers' work rules), and she handed it over to me. "You go do it, I'm done", she said.

I ran out with the Nagra and cornered the beast against the side of the house, where I finally got my snort on tape. It was only later that I learned that a javelina will gore you when provoked.

I was forced into another sound tech workaround when I was reporting a story on the Empire State Building for an NPR series called *Present at the Creation*, about American icons. I had found a daring electrical engineer named Tom Silliman who was the guy who changed the lightbulb on the pinnacle of the building. One time when I checked in with him on his cell a couple of weeks prior to our gig he answered, "Hey Pete, can't talk right now. I'm on top of the Sears Tower in Chicago."

We had arranged to climb as close as possible to the tippy top of the Empire State, where I would interview him. There is a fair amount of microwave radiation emanating from the upper reaches of the building during the day, when a number of television and radio stations are broadcasting via the antennae atop the structure. Therefore, we had to work in the middle of the night, when the signals could be powered down a bit.

It was a scene out of a 1950's sci-fi flick as we reached the room on the uppermost floor, where all the gauges were housed. Pasty-faced technicians with thick glasses and at least a few pocket protectors were excitedly moving very retro-looking dials back and forth.

From here, we would squeeze through a space and begin working our way outside and up ladders toward the base of the antenna, the one King Kong clung to before his sad plunge. But before we ever got that far, the sound engineer who was supposed to record the action for me announced that he couldn't go on. He was afraid of heights.

"Huh? But you knew we were going to the top of the Empire State Building. Why did you sign on?"

"I didn't realize we were actually going to go outside."

"Okay. You stay here. Give me the gear."

Tom and I shimmied our way onto a twelve-foot-wide metal grate called the ice shield. There was nothing between us and the shimmering lights of Manhattan but 1,300 feet of brisk New York air. My knees were knocking, and I had to hold onto the antenna to steady myself, but it was one of the more heart-stopping moments of my professional life. My acrophobic sound man had missed out on a truly dazzling sight.

I'll end this chapter with the story of a sweet but spacey tech who almost knocked us off the air. Back in the day on Friday nights, *Weekend Edition Saturday (WeSat)* staffers would stack up the reels of tape with our completed projects on a rickety typewriter table and then grab them when we arrived on Saturday mornings to put them on the air. We had been putting them on that table for years.

On this particular Friday night, our friend was strolling around collecting discarded reels after everyone had gone home. The process was to run a razor blade through the useless tape so the reels could be emptied and repurposed. For some reason only this engineer could tell you, he went after the reels on the typewriter table and sawed his blade clean through them all. We arrived at 5 a.m. to discover we had absolutely nothing to put on the air. It was the bad dream from which you could never awake.

We had two or three hours until broadcast time, and everyone pulled together. *Weekend Edition Sunday* offered us some of their completed pieces, and we got the correspondents on the line whose stories for Saturday had been gutted. Scott Simon interviewed them live about their reporting. Teamwork saved us from disaster.

# Chapter 12

# Convulsing Countries

## SOMALIA

One of my first shooting conflicts was almost my last.

In late 1992 into 1993, George H.W. Bush sent some 25,000 US troops to Somalia to try to bring order and to help the U.N. supply humanitarian aid to a place wracked by warring militias. I got there about eight months prior to the Black Hawk Down tragedy, when Somali militiamen shot down two Black Hawk helicopters. Eighteen U.S. servicemen were killed during the battle.

This was by far the most chaotic and dangerous situation I have ever found myself in for NPR and the time that I came the closest to serious harm. The country was in a complete state of anarchy (and regrettably remains much that way all these years later). Rival militias roared around the streets in what were known as technicals—pickup trucks with heavy caliber machine guns mounted on the beds.

Somalia was the only place I've ever been where you had to travel with armed bodyguards all the time. (To their great amusement, one day I joined our protectors in chewing khat leaves, the local preferred stimulant; it left me with a goofy green grin and the jitters.)

In countries where there's no functioning government credit cards are usually useless, so I was carrying cash, lots and lots of cash—around $32,000 in today's dollars—to pay our bodyguards, interpreter, fixer, cook, and rent, for the house in the capital Mogadishu we were sharing with the *New York Times*.

Usually, I stash travel money in three or four different places; so if I get robbed, I don't lose everything. On occasion, I have forgotten where one of those piles is hidden—under the mattress or was it between pairs of underwear?—and then it's a mad search to avoid an awkward expense report when I'm back in D.C. At the end of every day in Mogadishu, I would peel off hundred-dollar bills from my wad to pay the staff.

One morning we were awoken by the sounds of a firefight, and I rushed out with the reporter I was working with to cover it. It was early though, and our bodyguards and regular driver had not yet shown up for work. We grabbed another guy to drive for us and headed out to where we saw a helicopter hovering above a cement building.

By the time we arrived, things had quieted down although the helicopter was still thwacking in place. We stood around with a group of locals waiting to see what might happen. All of a sudden, there was a tremendous explosion and I reflexively went sprawling into the mud. When I looked up, the Somalis, so used to warfare, hadn't even flinched at the noise (which turned out to be a rocket fired by the helicopter) and just chuckled at the American goofball lying in the dirt.

Once the scene had played out, it was time to return to our compound. On the way back, we took a wrong turn and before we knew it, our car was surrounded by a group of Somalis angry about civilian casualties and Westerners who would soon return to their comfortable safe homes and forget all about them. Our driver stopped the car and froze. The mob expanded in size and was quickly growing more and more agitated. We screamed at our driver to *Go, Go Go!* But he just sat there.

Petrified in the back seat, I realized at some point that my feet were resting atop the AK-47 our bodyguard had left in the car the night before. It was an old rusty looking thing that I had no idea how to operate, and it probably didn't work anyway. I never seriously considered picking it up, but the mob was feeding on itself, shouting and beating on the car.

At some point, they got the back door open and started yanking me out. Just then our driver finally found the gas pedal and got us out of there. A few months later, in an eerily similar incident, four journalists in Mogadishu were dragged out of their car by a mob and stoned and beaten to death, their bodies mutilated. I consider myself a lucky man.

That close call figured into a decision I made a week or two later during a trip to the town of Baidoa about 150 miles northwest of Mogadishu. While I was there, I heard about a plan by some people to return to their villages in the countryside, which they'd fled because of fighting. I was offered an opportunity to accompany them, but the morning we were to depart my interpreter/bodyguard awoke with a malarial fever.

He was completely out of commission, and I had to decide whether or not to go solo. If we ran into an opposition militia on the road, I would be on my own and likely unable to communicate. I decided the story just wasn't worth the risk and after some agonizing, I let it go. I knew my editors in Washington would be okay with my decision. They would never push me into a situation I felt was too dangerous.

There was a happy ending to my Somalia assignment—a trip to Somaliland, in the northern part of the country.

While much of Somalia was colonized by Italy, Somaliland was once a British protectorate, and its people consider themselves autonomous from the rest of the country. From 1987-1989, the dictator Mohamed Siad Barre massacred tens of thousands of people there who resisted his rule. Now Somaliland was peaceful, according to a National Geographic photographer I met in Mogadishu. He recommended I visit and do a story about how it was free from the warfare that was convulsing the rest of Somalia.

I ended up catching a ride on a UN flight that was bound for Hargeisa, Somaliland's capital. As we were approaching the airport, the pilots received reports of fighting nearby, and the plane diverted. We ended up in the tiny country of Djibouti just to the north. I was upset that I wasn't going to get my story, but then I bumped into an interesting character at the Djibouti airport.

All these years later I can't remember his name, but he was a very friendly guy whose reading glasses dangled from his ears way down underneath his chin when he wasn't using them. He told me that he was from Somaliland and that the UN people were mistaken about the shooting near the airport. His country was completely tranquil and he insisted I visit. And he could get me there.

He happened to be the owner of a small airline; and if I met him at the airport the next day, he would put me on a flight to Hargeisa. There was something about my new friend that made me trust him. It was clear that he was very proud of his homeland and that he really did want me to get the word out that Somaliland wasn't like Somalia proper.

Sure enough, the next day I landed in Hargeisa. The city was pulverized from the bombing five years before. The customs office I stepped into was missing half its roof and the walls were riddled with bullet holes. But there behind a modest desk sat a smiling official who greeted me with a jubilant, "Welcome to Somaliland" and promptly slapped my passport with a stamp that read, "Entery." What a pleasure it was to spend a couple of bodyguard-free days just walking around on my own learning about the place.

My airline friend had told me that when it was time to leave, to give him a shout on the airport CB radio and he would send a plane my way. And so, one day there I was standing alone out on the tarmac looking up and watching as a jetliner came in for a landing.

I ran up to the plane and boarded. As I walked down the aisle and caught all the dirty looks from the other passengers, I realized that my guy had diverted this flight just for me and that people who had thought they were on a direct route to peaceful Nairobi, Kenya, were being forced to land in a war-torn place to pick up an American journalist. I felt guilty as I buckled up, but not too guilty.


## BOSNIA

Transportation also figured into a couple of landmark episodes during a trip to Bosnia and Herzegovina in December 1995. This was just as the nearly four-year siege of Sarajevo was ending and a peacekeeping force of 60,000 U.S. and NATO troops was entering the region.

I was traveling with NPR's fearless Pentagon correspondent at the time, Martha Raddatz, a veteran reporter of the Bosnian War with great contacts in the U.S. military. While we were approaching Bosnia from Germany, we got word that we needed to retrieve a satellite phone from our people already in country so that we could file along the way.

I was to hop on a US military flight from Germany, meet NPR reporter Andy Bowers on the tarmac in Tuzla, to the north of Sarajevo, grab the phone and jump on the same military transport plane back to Germany. The first attempt failed. As we approached the city, the cloud cover was just too dense and the pilots turned around.

A day or two later we made a second try, and this time we landed. For security reasons, the plane was not going to remain on the ground more than a few minutes before returning to Germany. This was one of those cargo planes where the back opens up for vehicles to drive on and off. Once we pulled to a stop, all my fellow reporters catching a lift disembarked, happy to have reached the action.

As the plane taxied down the runway preparing to turn around and take off, I made a mad dash to the side of the tarmac where tall, blonde Andy stood in a blue helmet, satellite phone case at his side. I said hi, grabbed the phone, and sprinted back towards the moving plane.

Observers must have thought I was completely insane, having at last made it to Tuzla only to freak out and try instantly to get away. I ran up the gangway into the now empty cargo hold of the slowly rolling aircraft just before the door shut and, still breathing hard, clutched my sat phone close as we flew back to Germany.

Soon after, Martha and I made our way with the phone to Zagreb, Croatia, and then on to a staging area along the Sava River on the border between Croatia and Bosnia, where US forces were assembling. Engineers were constructing a temporary bridge over which troops, tanks and other gear would enter Bosnia and continue on to Tuzla.

We were desperate to get to the Tuzla air base where the US military would be stationed, and one day Martha got word that there would be room for her the next morning in a US vehicle being ferried across the Sava. However, there was no space for me, so I was instructed to make my way back to Zagreb and then figure out a scheme to get to Tuzla.

Martha made it over the Sava and on to Tuzla as I returned to Zagreb and tried to make arrangements. If I could get to a particular gas station outside of Sarajevo, NPR reporter Tom Gjelten, who covered the war extensively and wrote a book about the siege, would meet me and drive us on to Tuzla.

First thing the next morning I went to the Zagreb Airport to find a flight to Split, Croatia, on the Dalmatian coast, from where I hoped to catch a car ride to that gas station. But it was Christmas Eve day and absolutely every plane was fully booked.

That evening, after I failed to make it standby on the last flight south, I got on a bus back to town for what I anticipated would be a very glum Christmas. Lucky for me, on the bus ride I fell into a conversation with the young woman next to me. It turned out she was in a similar situation, missing a chance to be with her family outside of Split for the holidays. I made a proposal. What if we shared a taxi for the 300-mile drive down the coast? I would pay two thirds. Deal.

I arrived at a hotel in Split around 2 a.m. and asked if they could conjure up a car and driver by 6 a.m., ready to head east to Sarajevo. A few hours later I stumbled downstairs to find Djani, pronounced Johnny, waiting for me.

He was not what I expected. With a bleached blonde buzzcut, white shirt, skinny black tie and a baseball jacket that read "Richmond High School," DJani looked like he had just arrived from a rave. Maybe he had. I dubbed him Johnny Split and thought he might make a good character in a Springsteen song.

He was determined to get me to Sarajevo on time, although the 1970 maroon Volvo he was driving did give me pause. Indeed, before we ever reached the famed 16th-century Old Bridge in Mostar, Bosnia, the muffler had fallen off; and we sounded like one of the NATO tanks we'd see on the road. Djani reassured me, "It's no problem." And it wasn't.

Winding down rain-slick roads, passing military convoys on blind curves, we listened to Pink Floyd and JJ Cale. Again, Djani reminded me, "It's no problem." He got me to the gas station outside of Sarajevo with time to spare. Hours later Tom pulled up in his jeep, with a Christmas tree strapped to the roof, and we continued on to Tuzla, where we joined the NPR crew enjoying Christmas dinner.

After reporting on the military in Tuzla, I made my way to Sarajevo—a place I'd never been—where the population was very slowly trying to recover from the siege by Bosnian Serbs that killed more than 5,000 civilians.

In that city, I reported a story on the Sarajevo Philharmonic's New Year's Eve concert, a triumphant event as residents looked forward to a coming year of peace. But the indelible moment for me from that time is driving in the car with our still-traumatized interpreter. As we pulled up to a main intersection in town he refused to stop because, he said, only weeks before this was a place where a Serbian sniper could get a clean shot at you.

# Chapter 13

# Hostile Environments

The first time I got killed it was from an iPhone wired to a hand grenade. It looked innocent enough lying in the grass so . . . I picked it up. That's when I saw the trip wire. WTF?

"You're dead," chortled the burly British former special forces soldier.

It was day one or two of my Hostile Environment Training. I was part of a group of about a dozen NPR reporters, producers and editors who had gathered at a summer camp in the Virginia countryside to learn the skills that would keep us safe in unsafe places: how to pass through a nasty checkpoint; how to recognize a minefield; how to apply a tourniquet; what to do when they drag off one of your colleagues. Will a cinder block stop a round from an AK 47? How about a brick wall? If you're kidnapped, do you try to make friends with your captors or keep a low profile?

At this point I had been in and out of hostile environments for NPR for about 30 years. Why they decided I finally deserved training I've never been exactly sure. I figured it had something to do with insurance. It didn't matter though. I was glad to do it. Really, it was a huge amount of fun, kind of like playing army as a kid in my New Jersey backyard, except with fake blood and low-powered explosives.

We were a jolly crew that included real war correspondents who had spent years and years in hot zones, unlike me who tended to sashay in and out of these experiences for brief periods of reporting before heading back to the safety of home. Each day we were drilled in techniques that could save our lives, from stopping a sucking chest wound to—well, not picking up an iPhone wired to a grenade. At night, we drank beer and played fierce games of ping-pong.

Some of the tips were a revelation. For example, did you know that a vehicle can be a bullet magnet? It draws fire; unless you are behind the engine block, your jeep might not stop a high-powered round. So when the shooting starts, if you can't drive away, get out of the car and run, for God's sake. As our British mentors leading the sessions told us, it is very difficult to hit a moving target, and most rebels have not had the benefit of extensive marksmanship training. That is why your odds of dodging a bullet are pretty good.

When you get to an unfriendly checkpoint, don't be friendly. Don't volunteer anything. Don't even roll down the window until they tell you to. The idea is to make yourself so much of a pain in the ass that the soldiers will want to get rid of you quickly and move on to the losers in the car behind you. Of course, like much of what we learned, everything is situational so this method might not work in every circumstance.

The Brits emphasized that rule pretty much number one is: Don't let them separate anyone in your group, especially a woman. You should interlock arms and resist as they try to drag her away. Only relent when it becomes apparent you will be shot if you don't.

Over the course of three or four days, we learned how to make an improvised stretcher using our shirts, how many chest pumps (30) to do to how many breaths (2) when performing CPR, and how to deal with the aforementioned sucking chest wound (try a Russell Chest Seal).

We were also schooled in how to exit as a group from an agitated mob scene and how much damage a heavy caliber machine gun could inflict. (A double brick wall might not save you; look for reinforced concrete, multiple stone walls or, preferably, find a dip in the ground). And we were told that during an abduction, at first you shouldn't make eye contact with your captors. Later, you can try to establish a relationship, but initially the kidnappers may be looking to make the point that they are serious by killing a hostage. You don't want to raise your hand.

By the end of the week, it was time for our final exam.

On graduation day, we convoyed in two vehicles along rutted dirt roads through the woods of the summer camp. The premise was that we were passing through rebel territory on our way to a "government press conference." After a mile or two, we came to a checkpoint manned by masked revolutionaries.

We were loose and jokey as they ordered us from the car, but soon things started to feel serious. One rebel (I am certain it was one of our instructors behind his bandana mask) started hassling me. He took my wallet and crappy Timex watch and shoved me around a bit. I was just hoping that he wasn't going to cram me into the trunk of the car, which I knew had been the fate of colleagues in previous classes and, of course, mobster Billy Batts in *Goodfellas*.

Then he tried to drag away our foreign editor. I dutifully interlocked arms with Didi and began a tug of war with the ersatz insurgent. Quickly, he cocked his weapon and put it to my head. Sorry Didi. See you later? Eventually, though, they released her and sent us on our way.

A bit further down the road we came upon a scene that had all the hallmarks of a minefield, so we swung wide. But lying in the explosive laden underbrush we spotted a sad victim. He was moaning and pleading.

"Help me, help me, please," he begged.

"We can't. We'll get blown up. But we'll send for help. Who do you work for?"

"Fox News," he uttered weakly.

In unison from both cars echoed, "Fuck you. You're on your own."

At the end of the road, we pulled up to a small campsite of cabins with about half a dozen people standing around waiting for the "press conference" to begin. As we got out of our vehicles and walked towards the clearing, a man in a checkered keffiyeh came running out of the woods screaming, "Allahu Akbar". This was immediately followed by a small explosion.

We all took off, running wildly through the forest. After a few minutes, though, we drifted back to a scene of carnage. Everyone at the campsite was on the ground oozing fake blood. (Side note: Fake blood is really tough to wash off. It stained my hands for days afterwards). Our mission was to minister to the victims' wounds and evacuate them, but we had to do it quickly. Another assault was imminent, our instructors told us.

I found a young woman lying in the dirt needing immediate assistance. Both of her legs were (wink wink) blown off, and the blood was spraying from the stumps like a busted water main. As I applied tourniquets to her limbs, she informed me that in addition to bleeding to death she was nine months pregnant. Terrific.

After she was stabilized, I began carrying her to our vehicle. Everyone stayed in character, acting like real bombing victims. At some point, the mother-to-be just couldn't resist. She knew I worked at NPR, so in the feeblest voice she whispered, "Do you know (former public radio talk show host) Diane Rehm?"

Finally, I was able to get her into our waiting minivan. Then we came under fire. Those nettlesome rebels had launched a second attack. I had to extricate myself from the bullet magnet, but mom-to-be was slouched against the door that was away from the gunfire. She wasn't moving and I just couldn't bring myself to trample on her in order to scramble out of the van safely, so I exited towards the incoming rounds.

Dead again.

Afterwards, during the exercise debrief, our combat professors told me that, indeed, I should have clawed my way over mom to get away. She was going to die regardless, they said, so my responsibility was to save myself. Harsh, but true.

Yeah, but she contributes generously to her member station.

# Chapter 14

# Kidnapped?

It was just a few months later that I was able to put my hostile environment training into practice. NPR sent me to Beirut with long time Middle East correspondent Deb Amos, who, coincidentally, had been in my group during the Virginia class.

We were on our way to Damascus to report on Syria's civil war. This assignment was a bit dicey, and I had never seen my bosses take our safety quite so seriously. We had planning meetings with a security consultant and were made to fill out a "proof of life" form.

This is a document you hope never ever is needed. It details what is to be done in case you are kidnapped. Do you want your family to be able to visit the region of the abduction? Would you like a press conference involving your parents? What special phrase will you utter in a kidnapper's video to indicate that you are being treated well (or the opposite?) Also included are some questions that only you and your family would know the answer to (my first dog's name was Cindy) in order to establish proof that, in fact, it is you they have snatched.

NPR also supplied us with poison gas suits and masks and gave us login aliases to thwart the Syrians from hacking into our company computer accounts.

The regime of Bashar al Assad kept our visas dangling though; and after about 10 days enjoying Beirut's bar and restaurant scene, Deb and I realized the Damascus trip wasn't going to happen. So we switched gears and decided to travel to Jordan to interview some of the commanders of the Free Syrian Army, the rebels trying to overthrow Assad.

Deb is an ace reporter and extremely well connected in the region, and we quickly moved up the rebel food chain to meet with ever more important leaders.

In one town, we found Commander Yasser Aboud. He was a former Syrian army officer who had defected and organized a rebel unit in the southern Syrian city of Dera'a. At one point, he was captured by regime forces, taken out on the street and executed. Except, just like me, he didn't really die. The bullet had passed through the bridge of his nose and taken out his right eye. He was left for dead but survived.

That event, he told us, had been captured on a cell phone video. Deb and I looked at each other. That audio would be great to include in the story. After the interview, he said, we could go to his assistant's house and retrieve it.

Once we finished with Aboud, we—Deb, me, our interpreter and the assistant who had sat in on the interview—headed out the door. As soon as we stepped outside, before I even realized what was happening, the assistant had swept Deb into his car and sped off.

Remember rule pretty much number one? Don't let them separate you from your colleagues, especially a woman.

I had failed miserably in my very first post-hostile environment training assignment and perhaps had put Deb in danger.

Our interpreter and I jumped into our car and tried to catch up to Deb's. We had thought the assistant's house was nearby; but soon we were driving out of town, and kept driving, for what seemed like forever. I was hyperventilating. Was he trying to kidnap Deb? This guy had been very quiet during the interview, speaking just a few words in Arabic. He seemed nice enough, but still. You could never be certain who was working for whom.

Mercifully, their car at last pulled up to a small house. Deb got out, smiling. I checked my underwear.

Turns out Aboud's assistant spoke fluent English. (It's always good to remember that you need to be careful about what you say in front of people you don't think understand you). Indeed, Deb had a few fearful moments herself during the beginning of the car ride, until her driver made it clear that he really was just taking her to his house.

Once inside, we had a lovely visit, got to meet his family and have tea. He wasn't able to find that cell phone, so we never did get the audio, but by that time it was beside the point.

There's a sad postscript to this story. A year or two after we interviewed Yasser Aboud, he and another commander we'd talked to on our trip were killed in Syria.

# Chapter 15

# Serving With Scott

I have covered three wars for NPR with Scott Simon. He and I have been joined at the hip for more than 25 years on *WeSat*. We're like an old married couple that finishes each other's jokes and stories. We're also the same age, with the same cultural references from *Gilligan's Island* to *The Godfather*.

Sometimes at our weekly editorial meetings I can feel the younger staff members struggling to keep themselves from flipping over backwards as their eyeballs roll back deep, deep into their sockets when Scott and I start in on one of our routines. Scott: "Leave the gun, take the cannoli." Me: "It means Luca Brasi sleeps with the fishes."

Scott has also come to expect the occasional absurd world leader song that I enjoy composing, never more than a line or two long—"Netanyahu that Netanyahu. He's such a wahoo, that Netanyahu . . ." Sung to the tune of *Old Man River*. There are also my half-baked get-rich-quick schemes I run by him, like *The Car Crapper—When You Need to Go When You Need to Keep Going* or the reality TV show based around competitive food storage skills called *Tupper Wars*.

But nothing bonds you to a colleague like spending time together in a conflict zone. Scott and I will always have that brotherhood. We also connected over the fact that we were old guys with young kids (and wives).

Having children dramatically changes the quotient of acceptable risk while on assignment. Once I had twins, I was simply less willing to do certain things I would have done before I was a dad. I would not enter the besieged city of Misrata during the Arab Spring uprising against Muammar Ghadaffi when I went to Libya. (Two world famous photojournalists were killed in a mortar attack in Misrata during this time.) And I didn't raise my hand to work from our Baghdad bureau during the darkest days of the civil war there.

When the girls were little, they didn't understand the hazards and didn't worry about me when I went off on assignment. But once they hit 10 or 11, I could no longer brush them off with a casual, "No, it's absolutely safe." They listen to NPR. They know what's going on. All I can do is assure them I will stay as safe as possible and not take any unnecessary chances—which is true.

Modern communication can make it easier and harder to be away from home. With a sat phone and computer I can connect with my family when I'm someplace unsavory. But at the same time seeing their faces makes me miss them all the more. I still remember how torn up I felt when my wife emailed me a photo of the girls on their second birthday, which I missed while I was in Afghanistan just after the U.S. invasion.

In 1999, Scott and I headed to our first conflict zone together—the NATO incursion into Kosovo. The Serbs were trying to keep the majority Albanian territory under their thumb, and things turned ugly. In those days, Scott was often the program host of choice to cover a war and I was his primary producer. His brilliant writing and uncanny sensibility made my producing look good.

A swarm of visiting journalists covering hostilities is often an opportunity for the locals to make some extra cash renting out their houses. In the capital Pristina, we fell in with a family that was happy to move to grandma's for a month to generate some rent money. Scott and I shared the room vacated by their two preteen daughters. We slept across from each other in frilly pink beds with a poster of Leonardo DiCaprio on the wall.

It was while away on this gig that I revealed to Scott that my wife and I were expecting twins. Scott, who cries during Budweiser com-

KFOR
**Press Pass**

Control #
3659

Name PETER BRESLOW

News agency NPR

Issuing office PRISTINA PIC

Issue Date 7/7/99    Exp. —

Holders signature

mercials, let loose with a torrent. Although I didn't know what the genders would be, Scott and I decided to come up with some names. I thought it would be a good idea to try out how they might sound when said aloud. "Brick Breslow, how do you plead?" seemed to flow right off the tongue.

We met a wonderful group of kids in the apartment complex where we were staying—all smiles and joking despite the war simmering around them. They were a welcome relief from the grim story we were covering.

Behind the apartment building there was a beat-up tennis court missing a net, but that didn't keep us from whacking balls back and forth with the children when we had some spare time. Amazingly, not too long ago, a young man recognized Scott on the street. It was Bini, one of the Kosovo kids, now a student getting his PhD in mathematics at George Washington University.

Scott is one of those people who is never not working. Usually on these assignments you are so exhausted after you've filed for the day all you want to do is watch a DVD of *Reservoir Dogs* and pass out. As I was doing just that, I saw Scott noodling away on his computer.

"Scott what the hell are you doing?"

"Oh, I'm just working on a screenplay."

That's Scott Simon. The man is also a caffeine fiend. He actually needs a cup of coffee in order to go to sleep. During the siege of Sarajevo when drinking water was scarce, he would shovel down dry spoonfuls of Nescafe.

My favorite story from our Kosovo trip was about the Fire Department in Pristina. The group was made up of both Albanians and Serbs, sworn enemies who occupied separate dorm rooms in the firehouse.

However, these men also pledged to uphold the firefighter's code to watch each other's backs. So when Scott asked an Albanian fireman if he would risk his life to rescue a fallen Serb firefighter during a blaze, he responded without missing a beat, "Of course." He saw no contradiction.

Indeed, when we went with them on a call, they worked as one team, hauling hoses and ladders and extinguishing the blaze. Afterwards, they returned to the fire station and their segregated dormitories.

My nitwit move on this trip came while we were out in the countryside reporting on displaced villagers. On the drive back into town, my bladder was bursting, so we pulled to the roadside, and I hopped into the underbrush.

The next day we visited a hospital to talk to some of the wounded. We found one man who was missing a leg. He told us that a few days before, he and his nephew had gotten out of their car to relieve themselves much like I had, except the nephew stepped on a landmine. Remarkably, the boy was blown straight up in the air, the man told us, but was not seriously injured. The uncle who was standing nearby lost a leg to the horizontally flying shrapnel. Ever since then, I have kept my peeing to the roadway in war zones.

# Chapter 16

# September 11 and on to Kabul

About a week after the 9-11 attacks, Scott and I headed to lower Manhattan. We thought there was no way we were going to be allowed to get close to Ground Zero, but we were mistaken. As we were hanging out at a roadblock some streets away, we bumped into a friendly state trooper who happened to be an NPR fan. Once he found out we wanted to get to the scene, he invited us to hop into his cruiser and drive there with him. We couldn't believe our good fortune.

First responders, firefighters, and the police were the heroes of the day; and as we drove towards Ground Zero, crowds lining the street held up signs saying "Thank You" and cheered for us. Scott and I just slunk down in the cruiser.

Just before that Ground Zero trip, I was sent to the site of the attack on the Pentagon to do a live Saturday morning interview with Scott, who was back in the studio. It was just supposed to be a scene setter, where I described what I saw at the charred section of the building. But Scott decided to torment me (live in front of four million people) and threw in a question about what my sources in the intelligence community were saying.

Of course, he knew I was as likely to have contacts in the intelligence world as David Duke was to have a B'nai B'rith membership; but I just winged it and escaped, without terribly embarrassing myself.

Scott and I have spent decades cracking each other up, including with emails that my wife fears someday will not only get us fired but brought up on charges. The email that almost did me in didn't go to

Scott, though. It was one I accidentally sent to most of the news staff. When we are chasing possible guests to book for interviews, we send out notices to alert the newsroom. A friend on staff sent one that named three Republican members of Congress he was hoping to book. Hitting "reply all" instead of "reply" I wrote something like:

*Oh, I have them locked in the trunk of my car in the parking garage. You want me to let them out?*

Thankfully, management chose to ignore the whole thing.

In early January 2002, Scott and I headed to Kabul. To get there we jumped on a UN flight from Islamabad. We made a nice gradual descent into the airport in Afghanistan, which differed from other flights I've taken into conflict zones. Landing in Luanda, Angola, during the civil war there, for example, the plane took a steep, almost perpendicular corkscrew death-dive to avoid any possible incoming missiles.

By the time we arrived in Kabul, it was more or less a mopping up operation with Taliban forces scattered. We had a great local crew on that assignment, including one of my favorite interpreters/fixers of all time, Zalmai Yawar.

Fixers are the people who make reporting possible in a foreign land. They might be a local journalist or university student or unemployed teacher. They know whom to interview, where you can get gasoline, and what road it's safe to travel down. And they can save your life.

With a driver and another fixer, there were five of us traveling around the country in a beat-up car, all wearing black NPR baseball caps. When we piled out for an interview, we looked like some sort of very minor league ball club.

Zally was an Afghan engineering student with the heart of a poet. I knew we were going to hit it off when Scott and I got to the house in Kabul NPR had rented for us to use as our bureau along with a couple of other news organizations. NPR's Jacki Lyden had been working there prior to our arrival and when her name came up, Zally said, "Oh Miss Jacki Lyden, she's a real party animal." She is, by the way.

Zalmai had survived a ghastly life in Kabul under the warring mujahideen factions. After his parents and sisters had fled south to Logar Province, where the family was originally from, Zally sat alone in his candlelit house, guarding the family's possessions from looters, teaching himself English by reading books he'd salvaged. Following the Taliban takeover, he had to endure indignities like being grabbed on the street for having hair too long and given an impromptu sidewalk scalping.

One day I noticed a brown spot in the white of his eye, and I asked what had happened. "Oh, it's nothing," Zally said. When I pushed, he finally told me that early one winter morning during the year he had spent watching over the family home, he was awakened by machine gun fire between two mujahideen groups.

As he tried to make it to safety in the basement, three mortar rounds landed nearby, one so close that gunpowder from it burnt his face and eye. To him, the whole event was barely worth mentioning. I would have been dining out on that story for decades.

Zalmai's fearlessness was just so casual. Soon after Scott and I arrived in Kabul, U.S. troops were set to play a friendly game of soccer against an Afghan team at the local stadium. Not too long before, black-turbaned Taliban had used this same arena for public executions, hanging their victims from the goalposts.

As Zally, Scott, and I walked towards the stadium, the crowd grew thicker and thicker. Soon we were smooshed shoulder-to-shoulder with hundreds and hundreds of people and I started to get nervous. Could there be a Taliban member hidden in the crowd with a bomb strapped to his chest?

As we pushed and shoved our way towards the entrance, I floated the notion that maybe this was not such a great idea, that we should just forget about attending the soccer match, and head home. Zally turned to me with a look of, *You have GOT to be kidding. We are finally free of the Taliban and you want to go home? We are going to this.* I felt like such a chickenshit.

Today, thanks to help from Scott and a few other people, Zalmai is a US citizen, with a PhD in geology from Indiana University. Just to reinforce his American bonafides, a couple of summers ago he worked at the Mammoth Site Museum in South Dakota, enlightening tourists about the largest collection of mammoth remains in the world, all with an endearing Afghan accent.

To this day, Zalmai and I remain good friends. He is heartbroken now that his country has once again fallen into the menacing hands of the Taliban.

Scott and I left the U.S. for Kabul on the day that *Wall Street Journal* reporter Daniel Pearl was kidnapped by militants in Pakistan, so we were a bit on edge. The tension increased when we realized that one of our soon-to-be departing housemates in Kabul was the *Journal*'s regional correspondent. They were pulling him out for safety reasons.

Scott and I wondered if the terrorists might have already zeroed in on him and his room in our house. Maybe they were planning another abduction. NPR or WSJ, what difference did it make? So, naturally, I let Scott have the WSJ bedroom when their reporter left.

Soon after, an Afghan who said he had helped Pearl showed up at our place. He was fearful that the militants were on to him and was frantic to flee the country with his pregnant wife. I never heard whether or not they made it to safety.

Electricity was in short supply in those days. When it was flowing you could either run the cheap Japanese space heaters that took some of the edge off the Kabul January frost, or you could turn on the lights. Not both at the same time. After a couple of weeks, I had had enough, and I told our foreign editor that I was going out to buy the biggest goddamn generator I could find. He said absolutely not. That wasn't in our budget. But he was far, far away in Washington.

Sometimes you just had to say screw the budget, like when I was told I couldn't fly business class on my way to Mogadishu to cover the conflict in Somalia. That was a place where when you stepped off the plane, someone might be trying to kill or at least kidnap you. I needed my beauty rest. Somewhere in my expense report I buried that high-priced seat.

Tea and Oreos with Scott Simon and the mujahideen,
Gardez, Afghanistan, 2002

For the generator, I went down to Chicken Street, the spot in Kabul where you could find just about anything you needed. I still have a warm place in my heart for our bright red Elemax SH 6000 that made life much more bearable that winter. Although soon after that purchase, the local electricity guy came by to say that for a small weekly "fee" he would make sure we always had current. He told us just to be certain we closed our shades at night so the neighbors didn't find out.

One day we headed south to the town of Gardez in Paktia province to report on a prisoner exchange between two rival militias. We interviewed the local warlord, Pacha Khan Zadran, on a windswept plateau. It was absolutely freezing and I lost all feeling in my hand holding the microphone.

After the interview, the warlord's brother took pity on us and invited us into his nearby hut. It was toasty warm, heated by a wood stove. I couldn't help but notice, though, that there was a rocket propelled grenade launcher leaning against the wall just behind the glowing stove. "Ah . . . is that safe?", I asked. The fighters smiled, and the RPG stayed right where it was.

To thank warlord Khan's brother for his hospitality, I broke out the Double Stuf Oreos I had purchased on Chicken Street. He absolutely loved them, and we spent an hour sipping tea and eating cookies.

Once it was time for the prisoner exchange, the parties quickly realized that they didn't have any paper on which to write down the names of the mujahideen to be swapped. Scott Simon to the rescue. He offered up his reporter's notebook, one of those handy narrow rectangular pads that can easily fit into your back pocket while on assignment. But this wasn't just any reporter's notebook. It was one from the Gay and Lesbian Journalists Association. Scott seems to have a lifetime supply of them, gifts for his generous work with the organization.

As the day wound down, the names of the militia men were dutifully inscribed in Scott's notebook; and off went these grizzled, battle-hardened fighters in vehicles bristling with 50 caliber machine guns and AK 47's, their leader clutching a notebook emblazoned with the motto, "We're here. We're queer. We're on deadline."

Probably our most powerful piece from Afghanistan was about Bamiyan in the central part of the country, where the Taliban had destroyed the two giant Buddhas carved into a cliffside. We even found a local Hazara man who had been dragooned by the Taliban to help with the destruction of the 6th-century wonders. But before that, we stumbled upon a poignant scene. There were two men out in a field unearthing the bones of one of the Taliban's victims. Some years before, one of these men had been forced to dig a grave and dump the poor soul into it, leaving the site unmarked. Now with liberation, the man had returned to give this anonymous person a proper burial.

We were lucky to capture this story. (I can still remember Scott's beautiful writing, describing a bit of spine that had been dug up as looking like a seahorse.) But afterwards, it was getting dark and cold; Bamiyan sits at over 9000 feet, and we had no place to stay.

We headed back into town where we found a guest house, but the place was full. However, once the owner spotted us, we could just see the dollar signs pop into his eyes and, before we realized what was happening, he started to boot out the guys lying around inside all comfy on their sleeping mats. They shot us dirty looks as they began filing out the door.

Thankfully, before things progressed too much further, a shiny black SUV pulled up to the guest house and in decent English one of the guys inside said, "Come on, you're staying with us." They were representatives of the local warlord who had heard there were some American journalists in town and wanted to host us. We ended up in a warm and cozy room padded with carpets and were treated to a delicious meal. Thank goodness, those other guys were able to return to their guest house for the night.

After about a month of reporting in Afghanistan, it was time to return home. We were going to drive east into Pakistan via the Afghan city of Jalalabad and then up through Khyber Pass and on to Islamabad. This was a nerve-wracking route. A couple of months before, the Taliban had murdered four journalists on this road.

We left in a two-car convoy just in case there was a problem with one of the vehicles. It was a cold day, spitting icy rain as we snaked down the mountainous switchbacks taking us out of Kabul. This was a white-knuckle ride for me, but not for my colleague. You see, Scott, who does not know how to drive, is a vehicular narcoleptic. As soon as you turn the key to the motor, he nods off. So as I peered over the cliffs reconciling myself to our certain deaths, Scott was dreaming about his first cup of Starbucks back in the States.

We made it down intact from Kabul and were humming along the

Jalalabad road when I spotted a gathering of men up ahead. As we approached, I sat on the edge of my seat peering through the rainy windshield.

My God, are they Taliban? No response from Scott, who remained in his caffeinated dreamland. To my great relief, as we got closer, I realized these were just herders with their animals. Once we arrived safely at the border, Scott awoke with something like, "Wow we're here already?" Yes, Scott.

For the last leg of the trip, we had to travel through the tribal areas of Pakistan, which were home to militants considered dangerous. The Pakistani military insisted a soldier accompany us in our car, but our vehicle was absolutely packed, no room for a guy and his gun. So before he could pull open the door handle, we sped off and left our soldier screaming at us in the rearview mirror.

Our trip had a literary finale. That evening in Islamabad we walked around the city and wandered into a bookshop. There, sitting on a table was a collection by children's author and *Weekend Edition* contributor Daniel Pinkwater. The book featured an introduction by none other than NPR's Scott Simon. Once the bookseller realized he had a quasi-celebrity in his shop, he quickly organized an impromptu intro signing.

# Chapter 17

# The Two Stooges
# of Baghdad

The next year Scott and I were sent to cover the U.S. invasion of Iraq. We arrived the week after residents toppled the statue of Saddam Hussein in Firdos Square. Here is the dispatch I sent back to NPR at the time:

Scott and I had it easy. The bombing of Baghdad was over and the shooting had calmed down by the time we arrived. The only thing nerve-wracking about our 10-hour drive into the city from Jordan was the fact that our driver did it pretty much without his hands ever touching the steering wheel. He brewed coffee from his cigarette lighter. He thumbed through his journal. He combed his mustache. He logged on to Match.com. The one time the gas pedal wasn't mashed to the floorboards was when we had to cross a bridge that had been cratered by bombs.

Our car was loaded with the supplies we'd purchased in Amman. While I was scouring the supermarket shelves there for dried fruit and bottled water, Scott was checking out the Dead Sea salt facial masks. And it struck me. I was headed to Baghdad with Frasier Crane.

We pulled up to the Palestine Hotel as the light was fading outdoors and non-existent indoors. No power, no elevator, and a garbage-strewn haul up 11 flights of darkened stairs to the room that had been heroically occupied for so many weeks by NPR's Annie Garrels, one of the few western journalists to remain through the allied bombing of the city.

The remnants of Annie's presence helped tell the story of her time in room 1133: helmet; gas mask and flak vest in the corner; a satellite phone with a broken antennae from when Saddam's security police made

a sweep and Annie had to stash the phone quickly; a big bowl of cigarette butts. (Sadly, Annie passed away in 2022.)

In front of the hotel sits a fleet of vehicles all sporting duct tape TV
insignias on their doors and hoods, as if those two letters give you some
kind of immunity. There was CNN's Humvee, ITN's fully-armored car, the
*Wall Street Journal*'s big white Mercedes, and NPR's little blue Toyota
(excellent gas mileage). Looking up to the 15th floor from the outside,
you can just barely pick out the balcony where earlier two journalists
had been killed by an American tank shell.

Beyond the vehicles, there was concertina wire holding off a throng
of desperate people: A man looking for news of his brother who disappeared in 1979; an out of work engineer who asks in perfect English,
"What can you do for me?" All we can say is that we'll tell his story to
the American people. Others ask if they can borrow our satellite phone
to call a sister in England or a mother in France to tell them that they are
alive. Almost all are passing notes explaining their situations to a little
kid who's collecting them in a cardboard box. Who is going to read them?

The one bright spot is a young man named Annis, who speaks English
with a slight southern accent. He tells me he spent time in Tennessee
and is now looking for work as an interpreter. We'll see about hooking
him up with a friend from the *Boston Globe*.

Stories throw themselves at you as you walk from the hotel. Go to
an emptied political prison and you bump into a former prisoner who
returned to see the cell where he was held and beaten. Go to a school
and you find a group of teachers who have spontaneously gathered to
clean up the glass from smashed windows and upright the desks for the
students they hope will return.

Once Scott and I had settled into our rooms at the Palestine, it was
time to hook up our satellite phone. We had limited-use cell phones
for quick conversations, but the sat phone would allow us to use our
computers and send high quality audio back to Washington. It was a
crucial piece of equipment.

Through the decades of my reporting overseas sat phones have evolved from enormous contraptions that required a technician to operate to sleek devices the size of a laptop. The one we had in Baghdad was somewhere in the middle, and getting it up and running became a Three Stooges routine, although in this instance there were just two.

First, I needed to set up the antennae, which was a three-panel winged affair that had to be anchored onto our tiny balcony and pointed towards the satellite at a precise angle. The Baghdad wind was blowing fiercely, so I tied down the thing with some nylon rope. To get the angle just right meant making micro-adjustments as Scott shouted out numbers over the roaring wind from a readout panel sitting on the desk in the room.

It was nighttime and, as noted, there was no electricity, so we were working by headlamp. We couldn't get things to function properly, so I used our cell phone to call Washington for instructions. But the cell reception on the 11th floor permitted only 20 seconds of connection before cutting off; so it was a constant sequence of redials as the tech person at headquarters would pick up the conversation where we had been interrupted and painstakingly walk me through the set-up process.

I followed the commands from a world away and tweaked the antennae as Scott continued to scream the numbers from the readout: "four . . . five . . . six (getting really excited, connectivity was reached at 10) . . . uh . . . four again (heartbreak) . . . seven . . . seven . . . we've hit seven," Scott shrieked. "10! 10! 10!" We were in business.

Orders came in quickly from Washington. Other news organizations were reporting on Saddam's secret documents. "You guys go track down some." And so we went searching, but we really didn't have to go very far, just to our neighborhood former Ba'ath party headquarters. There, we waded into a room knee deep in paperwork strewn across the floor.

Digging into the pile we pulled out reports detailing Saddam Hussein's spy network—a man claiming that his neighbor seemed suspicious, an account of someone saying that the dictator's eldest son Uday was an asshole. It was chilling to realize just how deep Saddam's tentacles spread. We also found a stack of Fedayeen certificates. These were awards Saddam presented to followers who pledged themselves to the destruction of Israel. The diplomas would come back to haunt us as we tried to exit Iraq.

Our driver during our time in the country was a petite dark-haired man named Ahmed. He diligently drove us around in his Toyota, finagling for gasoline and deftly negotiating roadblocks and highways pockmarked from artillery shells. He was also a man of deep compassion.

One day we went to an orphanage that was just getting back up and running. When the invasion started, many of the kids had fled this place where they had been abused and neglected. Now with the overthrow, some were drifting back to the only home they knew. We collected stories from the children and officials at the institution.

Once we were back in the car, I noticed that Ahmed was in his stocking feet. Usually, he wore loosely-laced basketball shoes. I asked him where they were. Turns out he had given them to one of the kids. "They have nothing," he told me. "I can get another pair of shoes." As Iraq continues to fall in and out of turmoil, I try to remind myself of that day with Ahmed.

After four or five weeks, our time in the country was over and we decided to head home the same way we had come in, overland to Jordan. I knew we had to be careful about what souvenirs we packed, especially those Fedayeen certificates. Scott and I each had grabbed a stack of them to present to our editors back in D.C.

The Jordanian border officials were on high alert and thoroughly checking the bags of everyone coming through because shortly before our departure, a guard was killed when a piece of ordinance being snuck out by a Japanese journalist returning home from Iraq exploded at the international airport.

Somehow Scott did not get the memo; and unlike me, who had buried the certificates deep in my suitcase, Scott had left his right on top so they would be the very first thing the inspector saw when he opened my host's bag.

It came to pass that as soon as the border guard spotted them, Scott was whisked away for further questioning. I looked around and he was gone. How was I going to explain this to my bosses when I returned to D.C. minus one significant team member? Uh . . . he was standing right next to me. Then he wasn't.

I frantically went searching for Scott amongst the offices at the crossing. The scramble ended when I opened a door and saw my friend serenely sipping tea with a customs officer. He had charmed the man who, after confiscating Scott's certificates, sent us on our way back home.

Our trip to Iraq ended in tragedy. We had convoyed into Baghdad with a reporter for the *Boston Globe* named Elizabeth Neuffer. She was much more familiar with the region than we were; so when she heard Scott and I were headed to Baghdad, she generously offered her expertise and companionship.

It was fun traveling with and getting to know her. She was so thrilled that she and her husband were starting the process of adopting a child. We didn't see much of Elizabeth during our stay in Iraq, but the day before our departure back to the US, we swung by her hotel. She was interested to hear that we had just come from Tikrit, Saddam Hussein's hometown, because she was planning a trip there in a day or two. Scott and I gave her what information and contacts we had. However, we skipped the story of our most foolhardy moment while in Tikrit.

As we wandered around that city, a group of residents came up to us to complain about how they had been treated by U.S. forces searching for Saddam. They said troops had tossed their homes as they searched for the on-the-lam dictator, and they wanted to show us. Scott and I said okay and we jumped into their car. As we got in, Scott whispered in my ear, "Remember Danny Pearl," who had been kidnapped and murdered by militants the year before.

From that moment on we were both on our guard, even more so as we walked into their darkened house and the door slammed shut behind us. (This was Saddam's birthplace after all.) Scott and I didn't need to exchange words to know that we both wanted to get out of there as quickly as possible. But it was a false alarm. These really were upset residents, not secret Saddam supporters. Still, Scott and I both exhaled deeply as we left their house and agreed never to share our idiotic move with anyone.

After our debrief with Elizabeth, we exchanged hugs and made plans to get together when everyone was safely back in Washington. Two days later Elizabeth Neuffer was dead. She was killed, along with her translator, when her driver hit a guardrail on the way back from Tikrit. It was heartbreaking for everyone who knew Elizabeth and a terrible reminder that many times it's reckless driving rather than gunfire that can kill you in a war zone.

# Chapter 18

# Deadline Pandemonium

The panic of an impending deadline you are sure you are about to blow can sometimes make you do astounding things, like the mother who is able to lift a pickup truck when her child is pinned underneath. At times, while editing with a razor blade, I would be so pumped with adrenaline that I couldn't hold my hand steady enough to cut the tape. I'd have to grab my right hand with my left to stifle the shaking. Today, while editing on a computer I sometimes get mouse quakes.

One day I was in a production studio madly mixing a piece for *ATC* with a sound technician as the clock to airtime ticked down. The show producer was hollering . . . "Are you gonna make it, are you gonna make it?" With the mix finished, I grabbed the metal reel off the tape machine while it was still spinning in rewind, gashing my finger.

I sprinted into the studio, blood dripping down my arm, desperately trying to keep it from getting on the tape. As I applied direct pressure to my hand, the piece was racked up and made it to air just fine. Listeners were none the wiser about the chaos lurking just behind the speakers on their radios.

To help keep the bedlam at bay, there was a dusty reel sitting on the shelf in the *ATC* area, containing a 20-minute piece about the Boer War by Neal Conan, a great host, reporter, and military history nut, who has since passed away. He had produced it just in case a day came when everything fell apart and there was nothing left to put on the air. The Boer War would give us a 20-minute reprieve to find some more content for the show. I don't believe that piece was ever broadcast.

With limited resources that paled painfully when compared with the big TV networks, NPR of the olden days could not jump on every story. Our motto was, *we'll do the piece two days late and call it analysis*. But sometimes our best work was done by the seat of our pants.

One afternoon in 1989 while *ATC* was on the air, I got a phone call from someone informing me that writer Edward Abbey, most famous for his environmental call-to-action novel *The Monkey Wrench Gang*, had died. That person told me we could do an interview with Abbey's friend, river runner Ken Sleight, who served as the model for the character Seldom Seen Smith in the book.

During our six-minute newscast, I pulled host Noah Adams out of the broadcast studio and got him on the line with Sleight in a production studio. Noah started the interview; but it wasn't going as quickly as we had hoped, and he had to get back into the main studio to read an upcoming intro. So I slipped behind the mic as Sleight was talking and finished up the conversation without the guest ever realizing he was now speaking with a different person.

With just minutes to air, I flew out of the studio and started frenetically cutting the tape. There was no time for me to write an intro. That task fell to Neal, then wearing his *ATC* executive producer hat. The problem was, Neal had never even heard of Edward Abbey. But he was a quick and elegant writer, so as I was editing the interview, I screamed out from my edit booth the salient facts about the author: novelist . . . essayist . . . environmental activist . . . wrote *Monkey Wrench Gang* and *Desert Solitaire*. Neal fashioned a touching script and our interview made it to broadcast.

Sometimes those quick turnaround obituaries don't quite work out. When Ernie Pantusso, who played Coach on the TV show *Cheers*, died, we were scrambling to find someone to talk about him on *ATC*.

Nosing around, I discovered that prior to his days as Coach, Pantusso had directed some episodes of another television classic, *Bonanza*. So I tracked down a phone number for Lorne Greene, who played the patriarch of the Ponderosa, Ben Cartwright. Greene was a bit hard of hearing and had difficulty understanding me when I called his office, so he said he would drive to his home, where he had some sort of audio enhancement device on his phone.

Great, I thought, and told the producer an obit for Coach was coming. When I reached him again about an hour later, Greene could hear me just fine, but he had no recollection of ever being directed by Ernie Pantusso. As a matter of fact, he seemed to know nothing about the man. We began making other arrangements for Coach's obit.

One obituary we were perhaps too well prepared for was that of our storied newsman Daniel Schorr. For decades while producing *WeSat* I worked with Dan, often overseeing his Saturday morning conversations with Scott Simon.

When Dan called you into his office for a chat—where until the end he worked on an IBM Selectric typewriter—he was affable enough, but you wanted to make sure to bring your A game. After all, this was a man whose career read like a history of 20th-century reporting, from his work with legendary broadcaster Edward R. Murrow at CBS, to his spot on Richard M. Nixon's "Enemies List," to his days at the founding of CNN, and well beyond.

As Dan moved into his 80's, we were all in awe of his stamina, his ferocious commitment to journalism and to remaining on the air. But at some point we had to ask ourselves: Can this go on forever? We decided probably not and began preparing Dan's obit.

Producing an obit while your subject is still very much alive is a bit tricky. You need to interview friends and colleagues and get them to sometimes speak in the past tense as they reminisce. Of course, the reporting needs to be done on the down low. This is especially critical when your obit subject is sitting in the office down the hall. The solution we came up with was a dummy title for the project, just in case Dan were to stumble upon it.

We named it Operation Buddy Hackett, after the Borscht Belt comedian. Why? Well, we had to call it something. But Dan outlived Buddy Hackett, so we switched slugs to Operation Buddy Ebsen, you know, Jed

Clampett of *The Beverly Hillbillies*. But, amazingly, just a week after Buddy Hackett's passing, Buddy Ebsen took his final dive into the *cee-ment* pond (as they called the swimming pool on the show).

As Dan moved into his 90's, people we'd interviewed for his obit started dying off. But we were happy to amend the story as Dan endured. Of course, just as it will for us all, time ultimately caught up with NPR's elder, elder statesman. Daniel Schorr died just shy of his 94th birthday in 2010, and his obit finally aired. There are still weeks during which the news is an awful, complicated mess when Scott will ask, "I wonder what Dan would make of all this?"

Chapter 19

# Show Producing

Deadline zaniness gets turned up a notch when you are the actual day-of show producer. We call it line producing. You (along with the editor and executive producer) are responsible for making sure the show has the right balance of serious and sad news and features. All the pieces of the program puzzle must make sense, flow together and properly fit into the time parameters.

There are exact time posts on the show clock that you have to hit so member stations can cut away from national programming and insert their local news, traffic and weather. Listeners often complain when they hear a program host cut short a guest during a live interview, but they don't appreciate the wrath that would come down on us from our stations if we were regularly to blow past the designated time posts.

There is an infamous *Weekend Edition* story of the lengthy taped interview Scott Simon conducted with Elie Wiesel. The piece preceding it on the air had run unexpectedly long, so as Scott tells it, with the time post fast approaching, the show director had to dump out of the Wiesel interview just as the renowned Nobel laureate was . . . very . . . slowly . . . saying, ". . . and the lesson of the Holocaust is . . ."

Then Scott jumped in live with, "And it's 18 minutes past the hour." We offended millions but kept our member stations content.

Minding the clock on a daily broadcast like *All Things Considered* is usually much more breakneck than on a once-a-week program such as *Weekend Edition*. I can recall days line producing at *ATC* when I had a landline phone up to each ear, an editor standing in front of me with a question, all the while trying to chew the bite of the sandwich I had in my mouth. It felt very unhealthy. One afternoon a reporter saw the harried look on my face and suggested, "Stop and smell the roses, man."

Then there was the stifling early June day in 1989 when the aftermath of the Tiananmen Square massacre was still reverberating in China, ten million Iranians were in the streets for the funeral of the Ayatollah Khomeini, and we had some kind of electrical outage. It was like the World War II movie *Das Boot*, about a crippled German submarine, as we tried to produce *ATC* with backup power that left us in half-light sweating through our shirts. We stayed on the air, though.

Line producing can become a constant juggling act over the course of the day, as pieces come in long or short, the story changes or news breaks. An editor might beg for more time for their reporter, or you may listen to a contribution from a freelancer and realize it is just too mediocre to put on the air. Sometimes there's absolutely nothing to replace that so-so piece with, so you wince and tell yourself it's only a radio program, and tomorrow we'll put on another one and people will forget all about it. However, these days everything lives forever in the digital world, so a lousy story becomes much more difficult to scrape off the bottom of your shoe.

The pace is more leisurely on the weekend, but in some sense the expectations are higher. With a once-a-week show, you want every piece to sing. I mean, you've had a whole week to put the thing together, right? I've had people say to me, "Gee, just one two-hour show per week? What do you do—show up to work on Friday or something?"

Ah . . . no. We spend every minute of our work week trying to craft the best program possible for the weekend. There is an art to it. How do you come up with a news angle that will not be completely played out by Saturday? Often, someone will pitch something mid-week that sounds terrific, but by Friday morning you might realize it has been talked to death.

In the age of Donald Trump, a Wednesday story that in normal times would have legs for a month—come Friday you hear yourself asking, "Was that this week?" because three other huge stories have intervened. Thus, you have to be flexible and willing to shift gears late in the process.

Despite all this, there are weeks when *Weekend Edition Saturday* and *Sunday* are, more or less, in the can when we go home on Friday or Saturday night and you are tempted to put things on cruise control. Inevitably, that's when the shit hits the fan. I have to admit that ever since 9-11, there is always just the faintest fear in the back of my mind that something awful is going to happen on my watch. More than once it has.

Around 3 a.m. on a Saturday in July 1996, my phone jolted me awake. (Unlike *Morning Edition*, *Weekend Edition* has no overnight staff.) It was a news editor calling from the office. She said, "You better get down here. There's been a bombing at the Olympics and it looks like at least one person has been killed." I rushed into NPR to start to figure out, with other editors and producers, how we would cover this story of what turned out to be an act of domestic terrorism—a bomb planted at the Olympic Park in Atlanta. We had a couple of hours to prepare, and NPR's continuous coverage ended up lasting throughout much of the day.

On a Saturday morning in February, 2003, *WeSat* was nearing the end of its first hour. We had our feet up and were starting to think about what to order for lunch. Then a producer looking at a TV screen said something like, "I think something weird is going on with the space shuttle." Pretty soon we, and the world, realized that the Columbia had disintegrated upon reentering earth's atmosphere, killing all seven astronauts onboard.

With the usual minimal staff that works on the weekend, we shifted into high gear—getting reporters on the line, booking experts. More recently, social media, especially Twitter, has helped us hugely in tracking down folks to interview during these calamities.

It's times like this when you really appreciate the true value of hosts like Scott Simon or Lulu Garcia Navarro or Rachel Martin or any of our other news magazine anchors. That day, Scott stayed on the air for hours (with maybe two pee breaks), interviewing guests on the phone we would put through to him, accompanied with just the barest of background information. It can be like a jazz riff at times, with the host vamping questions, probing to find answers when no one really knows exactly what has happened.

Often in these situations we bring in a "studio buddy" for the host, someone to help out with the interviewing and jump in when the conversation lags. On this day, it was one of our science correspondents.

During breaking news, the line producer must decide which pieces originally slated for the show to dump outright because they are too lighthearted, or which stories are just too important to kill. So, you try to find a way to keep them in the program. It's a tough call sometimes.

The key in these rapid-fire events is to triple make sure you are getting things right before you broadcast them. For cable news, it frequently seems like the top priority is to be first and then play catch up with the facts. I remember back in 1996 when TWA Flight 800 exploded minutes after takeoff from Kennedy Airport in New York that one cable network was reporting, *Absolutely!! This had all the hallmarks of terrorism.*

Ultimately, the National Transportation Safety Board determined that the disaster was most likely caused by a fuel tank explosion, not a terrorist missile.

NPR is extremely careful, but we've had our mistakes too.

One truly awful moment arrived on a Saturday morning in 2011 when U.S. Representative Gabby Giffords was shot in Tucson, along with 11 other people, by Jared Loughner. Six people died. At one point early on in our coverage, NPR reported that one of the fatalities was the Congresswoman. An NPR reporter had relied upon a usually reliable source, but in this case that person was mistaken. What's more, our reporter had not confirmed it with a second source, a mandatory rule in the newsroom.

Thank goodness Gabby Giffords survived, but the upset we caused even after we issued an on-air correction was profound, for the family and for Scott Simon, who is friends with Giffords, and her husband, former astronaut and now U.S. Senator Mark Kelly.

On another weekend, I was doing my usual groggy Sunday stumble into the newsroom at 6 a.m.—the show completely ready to go, my thinking on autopilot—when a newscast producer called out to me, "There's been some sort of shooting in Orlando . . . not sure yet how bad it is." It was at the Pulse Nightclub, and it was very bad. Forty-nine people were killed and dozens were injured. Over the next few hours, as the scope of the tragedy became clearer, we increased the story's presence in the show.

Ultimately, we went into special coverage. That means after notifying the stations what we were up to, we threw out the normal *Weekend Edition* segmented clock and entered a realm where there were virtually no time posts to hit. As guest host Linda Wertheimer commanded the anchor's chair, additional editors, producers, reporters, and bookers were brought in to assist the *WeSun* crew.

It wasn't seamless. There was some confusion about what theme music we were supposed to use for special coverage and who would do exactly what. Should one person write all the copy? Who is talking to the police? Can we get someone in the studio to give Linda a break? In the end, we held the air for hours and hours.

There is a tremendous sense of responsibility during big news events. We are telling millions of people what we believe are the facts and what they need to take away from a sometimes history-defining moment.

Everyone pitches in—finding an eyewitness, calling sources, tracking down an important piece of audio, even ordering pizza for people who are too busy to eat. It is chaotic. It is exciting. And it is so important.

When it's over, we're off the air and the adrenaline quits pumping at light speed. You feel like you've been drained by Dracula and slammed by a dump truck at the same time.

# Chapter 20

# Disasters Natural and Otherwise

Sometimes our newsroom mini-catastrophes are due to operator error. Case in point: One weekend an editor had baked some delicious sticky buns for the staff. Man, they were good, especially at 6 a.m. Well, a guest host, who shall remain nameless, was savoring hers throughout the morning and brought one into the studio to nibble on during the show.

Now there is a reason they are called *sticky* buns. Our host managed to get some icing on her scripts and a couple of the pages sweetly glommed together. When her mic light flicked on, she could not find her copy to read, which hid glued to the previous script.

For a full never-ending minute, millions of listeners out in radioland—perhaps enjoying their own sticky buns—were treated to the "ums" and "ahs" and paper shuffling of our news reader as she scrambled to find her place, which she never did. Once we realized the situation was absolutely hopeless, we threw in the towel and just went to the audio tape.

In another instance a long, long time ago, a newscaster was running late and sprinted into the studio with his script just as they turned on his mic. He opened his mouth to read, but he couldn't catch his breath. What came out on the air sounded like a man having a heart attack, which is what drove concerned listeners to call in, God bless 'em.

It's a good thing there are three feeds of all our news programs across time zones; by the time people in Spokane hear us, we've usually fixed all our mistakes and listeners think we're flawless. If only.

Deadline lunacy has never been limited to in-the-building work. Very early on in my career I went with an NPR team to cover the United Nations World Conference on Women being held in Nairobi, Kenya.

During our first attempt to file back to headquarters, we tried to use the lobby telephones in the conference center despite the fact that there was a large sign warning something like: *These telephones are not to be used by journalists.* Admonishments don't always work so well with reporters.

As I stood guard, NPR reporter Mike Shuster (who died in 2023) unscrewed the mouthpiece of one of the phones, used alligator clips to attach the phone to his tape machine, and began feeding the audio down the line back to Washington. It was not very long before a security guard came by and, despite my efforts to rope-a-dope him, quickly figured out what we were doing and furiously booted us out.

We decided to head back to our hotel to file, using a device called a Rood, which required two telephone lines. The only way we could get the thing to work was to place it in the hallway between our two adjacent rooms and run cables from the machine to the landlines in each room. However, the way things were wired, Mike in one room could hear what people on the phone from D.C. were saying, but they couldn't hear him when he talked into his receiver. At the same time, I, in the other room, couldn't hear Washington's instructions on my phone, but somehow they could hear me.

So Mike, through his open door, would yell to me something like, "They say they need more gain (volume)"; and I would turn things up and ask back to D.C. on my phone, "How's that?" They would tell Mike, "No, you need to crank it up a bit more"; and Mike would relay those commands from his room to mine.

This went on and on into the night. At one point, some confused Kenyan hotel guests walked by, witnessing this contraption in the hallway and two guys screaming at each other from room to room. That's when one of them asked, "Is this some sort of experiment?" Actually, it kind of was.

A few years later, correspondent Linda Wertheimer and I experienced the madness of filing from back-to-back natural disasters. We were dispatched to San Francisco the day after the 1989 Loma Prieta earthquake. The 6.9 magnitude quake killed more than 60 people and caused billions in damages. Linda and I wanted to report on the collapse of a double-decker freeway in Oakland, where a great number of casualties had occurred.

This was pre-GPS, so as I drove through the hilly San Francisco streets on our way to Oakland, I unfolded a map across the steering wheel. With a *this isn't going to end well* look on her face, Linda did her best to keep the map from flapping in my face.

Somehow we made it to Oakland and back intact, and then furiously put the story together in our semi-functioning earthquake-battered hotel rooms. These were still the days of reel-to-reel tape; so once we finished, I dashed out of the hotel and headed for our member station KQED, where I had never been, to transmit our story back to Washington.

Slamming through the front door of the station with the tail of the tape trailing behind me, I screamed to the receptionist, "Where is the uplink?" She had no idea who I was or what I was up to, but she pointed me in the right direction and we (just barely) made our deadline.

After that assignment was over, Linda and I were told to head immediately from California to southeast Texas to cover another natural disaster, major flooding. On our way to the airport, we found a sporting goods store where we could buy tall rubber boots.

Before we knew it, we were in an outboard motorboat with a husband and wife heading up the Trinity River to see how badly the flood had damaged their home. As we skimmed over the engorged waters, we had to duck our heads to avoid smacking into giant balls of fire ants clinging from low hanging branches.

Once we reached the house, our boots were pushed to their knee-high limits. The homeowners warned us to be on the lookout for water moccasins, which would be active in the flood waters, even inside the

house. Our sound technician, John Carillo, had to concentrate on holding his two microphones and really couldn't look around; so when a
branch floated by and brushed up against him, he feared the worst. In
the moment, Linda and I had no idea that our diligent and dedicated
engineer was just waiting to feel the sting of fangs in his thigh.

# Chapter 21

# South American Sojourn

I left New Jersey for college and barely looked back. I finished up my degree by student teaching at an American school in Quito, Ecuador, which was kind of a way to get me to South America, where I had always wanted to travel. I didn't realize it then, of course, but this journey would pave my way into NPR.

I did have a Latin American experience some years prior that first aroused the travel bug in me. In 1967, the Summer of Love, I went to visit my friend Alan in Los Angeles.

It was a magical time when I first heard the long version of The Doors' *Light My Fire*, saw The Yardbirds, Buffalo Springfield, and Captain Beefheart live, got a glimpse of marijuana for the first time, and grew my hair a little long. After I returned to New Jersey, I was (very briefly) the coolest kid around.

Towards the end of that summer, I traveled with a group of teenage California boys on a YMCA Surfin' Safari outside of Ensenada, Mexico. My friend Alan and I were the cooks. For 10 days we slept on the beach; and when I wasn't frying eggs or scouring pots, I learned the fundamentals of surfing. When we ventured into town, it hit me—there was another world out there filled with sights, smells, sounds and language nothing like in Bergen County, New Jersey.

Nine years later I landed in Ecuador and it was transformational. While there, I managed to climb Mt. Cotopaxi, at 19,347 feet considered by some measurements to be the world's highest active volcano. I took ayahuasca with a shaman in the jungle, swam in a lake packed with piranhas, and balanced on a wooden stool that was added last minute to an overloaded bus for a nightlong ride from the Amazon to the capital, all the while reading *The Brothers Karamazov* by flashlight. I also got to watch Mel Brooks' *Blazing Saddles* in a Quito movie theater filled with Spanish and Quechua-speaking locals who I don't think quite got the humor of a Yiddish-inflected American Indian.

One of my high school students in Quito was the son of the U.S. ambassador. The kid wore mirrored sunglasses in class and wrote "Fuck Ecuador" on the top of his homework assignments. Apparently, he was a bit resentful that his father had been transferred from sunny Rio de Janeiro to the chilly Andes.

That New Year's Eve the ambassador was throwing a party at his residence, and his daughter was coming down from college in Boston. "Would you like to attend?" asked the ambassador's wife on the phone, perhaps thinking her daughter and I might hit it off. "I'm calling it black tie. Do you happen to have a tux?"

My wardrobe of jeans and flannel shirts emphatically did not include a cummerbund, but Mrs. Ambassador said not to worry. Her husband had several tuxes and I could borrow one. A few days before the gala I visited the residence, where a housekeeper showed me to the ambassador's bedroom closet. He really did have a bunch of tuxedos, so I grabbed one and a pair of shiny black shoes, too. Everything kind of fit.

Early New Year's evening I am dressed, pleasantly stoned and almost ready to head out when the telephone rings. It's the ambassador himself inquiring about the label in my suit jacket. I told him what it said, and he ordered me to get to his place ASAP. I had walked off with his best tux, the one he was planning to wear that evening. "Hurry, guests are arriving."

At the mansion, I was whisked into the bedroom where the ambassador was standing in his boxer shorts and some very impressive over-the-calf black socks. I gave up my suit, put on another and headed down to the party.

As the 26-year-old son of a luncheonette magnate, I had never been to anything remotely as elegant as this: servants, a grand ballroom, chandeliers, flowing gowns, and, it seemed, my own waiter, who made sure my champagne glass remained topped off. I kept him busy.

The evening progressed nicely and the ambassador's daughter and I were percolating pretty well, almost as well as my waiter and me. Things started to falter, however, when we decided to dance. I was a bit too enthusiastic with my spins; and after the second time I flung my date sprawling across the dance floor, she suggested we move to a side room and take a breather.

The next thing I remembered was waking up slumped in a chair. It was about 3 a.m. The mansion was dark, quiet, and empty downstairs—and I was all alone. I slunk out the front door and stumbled home to my apartment. I was not invited back.

After that teaching gig, I hit the road, traveling on the cheap. I worked my way down the spine of the Andes, hiking four days in freezing rain at 13,000 feet along the Inca Trail to Machu Picchu—a bucket list destination if there ever was one. Later on, I found myself chewing coca leaves (which were legal) while passing through Bolivia during a two-day train trip to Chile.

That train was so crowded with people sitting in the aisles and everywhere else that there was no way to get to the bathroom. So I must confess that at one point on the journey I snuck between cars and, holding on for dear life, swung my butt out over the Altiplano and fertilized the Bolivian countryside.

My travels continued, hitchhiking through the driest place on earth, the Atacama Desert, then on to southern Chile and through the Straits of Magellan. A month later I thumbed my way into Argentina's Patagonia region and continued north.

Once I reached the capital of Buenos Aires, a fellow traveler I knew spotted me on the street. "You better get to the Embassy," he said. "I saw your name written on a chalkboard there."

Oh, my God, someone has died.

At the U.S. Embassy, there it was in black and white, *If you know the whereabouts of Peter Breslow, please contact this office immediately.*

It turned out that my parents had reported me missing. The pre-internet letters I wrote took a long time to arrive by airmail from Patagonia to River Edge, New Jersey, and my mother and father had gotten worried.

A lot of people went missing in South America back then, so my folks weren't totally out of line to fret. When I was living in Quito, my roommates were supposed to meet up with a traveling American couple. They never showed. Their families, not finding the Ecuadorian authorities responsive and frustrated by the U.S State Department's efforts, hired someone to investigate.

The detective, who told me he was originally in the country to collect plant specimens from the jungle, ended up using my little cassette recorder to tape an interview with the chief suspect, a landowner from the Cuenca region who was seen with the couple in that city.

The landowner was one of those people you sometimes meet when traveling cheaply, a local who speaks your language and is just a bit too helpful. In those instances, you have to trust your instincts as to whether this person is out for something more than simply your friendship.

When nothing came of the detective's investigation, my roommates and I headed south to Cuenca to do our own sleuthing. We followed the suspect around for a bit, tailing him into a bar and restaurant. I really don't know what we were thinking. Of course, our surveillance turned up nothing; and the American couple, as far as I know, was never found.

In Buenos Aires that evening, for only the second time in a year I spoke to my poor parents on the phone. I assured them all was well as my mother pleaded, "Haven't you had enough of all this wandering?" Not quite.

There had been another frenzied phone call moment with my parents years earlier, after quitting college, while I was hitchhiking around the U.S. with my buddy Chris. During this walkabout, I would call my folks (collect) every two weeks. One time I was checking in and the first words out of my mother's mouth were, "Did you hear who died?"

"What? Oh no, who? Uncle George? Aunt Hermina?"

"No, Dan Blocker."

"Wait, you mean Hoss Cartwright from *Bonanza*? Why are you telling me this?"

"I don't know. I thought you'd want to know."

That was my mother—a fiery Hungarian beauty who would occasionally go off the deep end—one day stuffing my adoring friends with Oreos and milk after school, and the next rampaging after me and my sister Susie with a wooden spoon or sometimes a belt (sister Linda was older and mostly able to escape the mayhem).

During my gallivanting, Argentina was in the depths of its "dirty war" against leftists. My long hair and army fatigue jacket made me suspect. But aside from a strip search and some menacing appraisals by the military police, my U.S. passport kept me from getting thrown into the back of one of the notorious unmarked Ford Falcons the cops used to cruise Buenos Aires and disappear suspects.

That strip search occurred in northeastern Argentina on my way to Iguazú Falls on the Brazilian border. Once I got my clothes back on, I made my way to a dog-eared campground at Iguazú. It was run by a German guy and, this being Argentina in the 1970's, I kept wondering if I had stumbled upon Dr. Mengele. But he proved harmless, so I pitched my tent and settled down in the lush countryside, awaking each morning to an glorious fluttering display of iridescent blue morpho butterflies.

This section of Iguazú had seen better days and the tourist infrastructure was pretty downtrodden, but that was fine with me. Every day I would pack a lunch, grab my book, and sidestroke across an inlet of the Iguazú River with my stuff elevated above the water. On the other side was an island that was once served by small boats. But all that remained of its more popular days was a flight of moss-covered collapsing stairs that led to the upper part of the island.

Following the steps, I came upon a lagoon that was fed by a 20-foot-high thundering waterfall. I had the place to myself. Sitting underneath the falls I could just barely withstand the pounding, occasionally wondering who would find my decomposing corpse if a log happened to cascade down on top of my head. I visited the island for close to two weeks. Then I hit the road again, for Brazil.

According to the gringo grapevine of travelers, you could make good money teaching English in Rio de Janeiro; so that's where I landed, bearded and broke.

I lived in many spots in that city. One that was short-lived was the House for Students, a huge pink and white mansion in the Flamengo section of town. It was a ramshackle place with peeling paint and poor plumbing full of budget travelers. I showed up one afternoon, threw my backpack into an assigned room and promptly went to a bar. I returned late at night a bit loopy and had absolutely no idea which was my room in the warren of doorways.

I stumbled around trying doorknobs until I found one that turned. Inside some guy was sleeping, but there was an empty bunk opposite him. It had no mattress, just wooden planks; at that point, it would have to suffice.

Trouble was I had to pee like a racehorse. I was afraid of losing my way back to the room if I went out in the hallway looking for the bathroom, so what the heck, I would relieve myself in the sink. But, oh, that plumbing. The pipes weren't connected and my flow ran right onto the floor. I halted midstream and finished my business out the window.

At this point, though, my roommate awoke to find this non-Portuguese speaking stranger in his room. Hearing the ruckus, the night watchman showed up and wanted to kick me out. My roomie turned out to be a nice guy and persuaded the guard to let me stay until daylight, when I was able to locate my rightful room.

From there, I moved into a boarding house with four or five other guys and a matron who called me Pepe. She was very excited to have an actual American join the crew. "Oh, Pepe, I hope you'll be happy here."

One of the residents slept in the kitchen on an extended shelf above the washing machine. Every morning when I walked in there to make my coffee, he swung out from his bunk declaring, "Estou em uma guerra." By the time I moved out, I had learned enough Portuguese to understand what he was saying, "I am in a war." Sleeping on top of the washing machine in the kitchen, yeah, I guess so.

My fantasy of helping bikini-clad girls from Ipanema improve their English never did materialize; mostly, I instructed businessmen. I remained in Rio for about a year teaching before departing to explore the country's fabulous remote beaches, its exotic Northeast and, finally, the Amazon. The tropics made it easy to stifle my occasional worries about what I would do when all this screwing around someday came to an end.

# Chapter 22

# Waiting for Lefty

While I was traveling in South America, I had been corresponding with a kind of girlfriend named Midge. Out of the blue she said she wanted to come visit me in Brazil. Sure.

After saying goodbye forever to my Rio girlfriend Grice (we are Facebook friends today), I met up with Midge in the colonial city of Salvador. From there, we decided to work our way further north to Belém at the mouth of the Amazon and then travel up the river to Colombia. But things didn't go well, nothing remotely close to well.

On our way up the coast, while camping together on a deserted beach, thieves made off with most of my Rio savings. They took my passport too. The US consulate quickly got me new documents, but the Brazilians didn't like my shaggy looks, and they would only give me 10 days on my visa before I had to be out of the country. We were about 2,500 miles from the border, traveling overland and by river, so that was one deadline I was not going to meet.

Next, I came down with hepatitis A. Prior to Midge's arrival, I had been camping by myself mostly naked for a month or so under the palms on an empty beach just downstream from a little village. There I learned to monkey squat my way up coconut trees, hack open the coconuts with a machete and turn the dried shells into bowls—à la Robinson Crusoe—all the while bodysurfing waves that were just shy of being able to kill me.

I thought I was purifying that stream water with iodine tablets, but apparently the pills had expired and a month later I was left jaundiced and too weak to walk. As I languished for weeks in a hammock, Midge was getting antsy. This wasn't what she'd signed up for.

Finally recovered, I continued on with Midge, hitchhiking towards Belém. One day we got a long lift from a trucker. Around midnight he was turning off our route, so he dropped us off at what could charitably be called a truck stop.

We decided just to pitch my tent by the side of the road and make the best of it. As we were settling in for the night, we heard approaching voices. I peered through the tent flap and saw three strapping guys moving towards us. They're going to kill me and rape Midge! Squatting inside, I grabbed my machete, trembling as the men drew closer and closer. I wasn't going down without a fight. Now they were standing right in front of the tent. I braced myself.

"Hi," one of them said in Portuguese. "What's going on?" I explained our situation. "Oh, we were just wondering," he said. "Have a nice evening."

A few days later we made it to Belém and bought tickets on a small banana boat heading up the river that evening. That afternoon I swung by the U.S. consulate, which provided mail service, to see if anything had arrived for me. There were no letters, but there was a telegram from my childhood friend Lefty Monahan. (Remember that MG Midget rolling down the lawn?) He was getting on a bus in Rio for a 56-hour ride to meet me in Belém. Please wait for him, the telegram read. What the? I had no idea Lefty was even coming to Brazil.

By this point, Midge and I had spent almost two months stalled in the country. There was no way we could postpone getting on that boat. I left Lefty a note at the consulate telling him we would meet him in Manaus halfway up the river.

Travel on the waterway was endless. The Amazon was in flood and we were headed upstream. I truly could have walked faster. There were stifling days spent staring out at the brown water, wide as a huge lake, and the green ribbon of jungle that bordered it. The only wildlife we spotted were some pink Amazon River dolphins.

At night people slung their hammocks up on the deck to sleep. It was packed. There were bodies swaying above, below, and on either side. If you needed to get up during the night, you had to crawl on your stomach under these human sausages to get to the bathroom.

By the time we made it to Manaus, Midge had enough. She got on a plane back to the States. I was crushed, but I really couldn't blame her. It had been a shit show. I smoked some of the first cigarettes of my life as I watched her board her flight.

I spent the next two weeks waiting for Lefty in Manaus at the cheapest place in town, the Pensão Tropical. It was the end of the line. For $1.50 a night I shared space with glassy-eyed travelers who had spent too much time in the tropics and a former Tupamaro guerilla from Uruguay hiding out from the federales. He showed off what he said was a bullet hole in his leg. Oh, and my visa was well-expired by this point. I was no longer legally in Brazil.

My room at the pension was a windowless closet with a bunk bed and a tiny fan. My roommate, sleeping above me, was a baker who got up every morning at 5 a.m. to go to work, which was pretty much the time I, battling insomnia, was finally falling asleep. We did have a third guest who visited a couple of nights a week—some kind of gigantic Amazonian rat. More than once I awoke with the thing nibbling on my toes.

Since I was recovering from hepatitis, I couldn't drink; so getting loaded wasn't even an option. If only I were a great novelist, I thought, I could really turn this into something: *A Jersey Boy's Heart of Darkness*.

I did have just enough money (the beach thieves had left my travelers checks) to get on a cheap flight back to the U.S., but I was determined not to end two years of life-changing travel in South America on such a sour note. I just kept telling myself that if I could make it through this, I would be able to make it through anything else for the rest of my life.

After about a week, I was desperate to get out of Manaus. I'd heard about a campsite on a river beach not too far away, so I hopped on a boat across the confluence of the sandy Amazon and the dark Rio Negro and then took a bus to a small village. I arrived at night and pitched my tent at the first empty spot I found.

In the morning, I awoke to small ants crawling all over me. Flailing like a lunatic, I jumped out of my tiny blue mountain tent, sweeping the bugs off me. When I looked up, a curious crowd of locals was surrounding me. Turns out I had bedded down in the town square, where residents had gathered to see who or what would emerge from the sleek space-age nylon thing that had landed among them during the night.

Outside of the village I found what seemed to be a kind of ruined picnic spot. There were a couple of broken-down thatched-roofed lean-tos abutting a murky pond. Not Club Med, but I set up my tent, cooked some rice on my camping stove and went to bed.

In the middle of the night, the skies opened up with a tropical downpour and my tent collapsed. Wretched is too gentle a word to describe things. I gathered up my soggy sleeping bag and went and sat under a thatched roof until daylight, when I headed back to Manaus. Then I dropped off a note for Lefty at the local consulate, telling him that I was heading further upstream. "Please, please, meet me at the border in Leticia, Colombia. I need a friend."

Soon I was back on another pokey banana boat chugging upriver, having no idea what awaited me when I would present my passport with its expired visa at the border.

I really didn't want to repeat the experience I'd had months earlier when I had been held for a day in a Rio jail after being misidentified as a drug trafficker and arrested at gunpoint. The friend I was picked up with that morning suggested we try to escape once it got dark. I told him I thought that would likely end badly.

No one knew we had been grabbed, and the police wouldn't let us get a message out. This was still the era of military dictatorships, remember, and that evening the cops drove us up into the mountains outside Rio. We were headed to the police interrogation center, where we were certain the door prize was electroshock to the genitals.

After some tense moments at the facility, the cops somehow realized their mistake. We were not drug dealers. The air now cleared, the policemen patted us on the back and let us go. No harm, no foul.

Back on the Amazon, in this era of human rights abuses, who knew what the authorities at the border would do to me for overstaying my visa?

I spent two more interminable weeks chugging up the river, trying to keep sane by listlessly reading in my hammock Henry Miller's *Tropic of Capricorn*, or maybe it was *Tropic of Cancer*. (Wait, wasn't I in the Tropic of Capricorn?) Ultimately, I reached the frontier. For all my nervousness about my expired visa, the Brazilian immigration official in Tabatinga barely glanced at my passport as he stamped me out of the country. The problem arose when I walked a couple of blocks and tried to enter Leticia, Colombia.

"Where is your tourist card?" the border agent asked.

"What card? I thought you could just enter Colombia."

"No, mi amigo, you need a tourist card, and you can only get it outside the country at the Colombian consulate back down the street in Brazil."

But the consular offices were closed for the weekend, and then there were national elections; so the earliest I could get a stamp would be four days later—four days in no man's land, exited out of Brazil, but not officially entered into Colombia.

I bided my time in town hoping Lefty would show. There was a disturbing strangeness to those days: a couple with a monkey who tried to befriend me, but seemed like they were capable of pickling and storing me in a 50-gallon drum in their basement; and a guy walking around in a leopard-print speedo who called himself Tarzan.

One day, though, sitting in a cafe nursing a fruit drink, I saw a familiar gangly figure amble past. I ran out and hugged Lefty. I was never so happy to see someone in my life.

After that, things improved quickly. I got my tourist card. Lefty and I discovered that if you greased the palms of two roly-poly local pilots, you could get yourself a ride in a DC-3 bound for Bogotá from Leticia.

The next day we found ourselves in the seatless cargo hold of the old plane lying atop cardboard boxes packed with little plastic bags full of water and live tropical fish. There were also cases and cases of some off brand Cheez Doodles. Our pilots made their way through the hold to the cockpit by tromping on these boxes, occasionally crashing through, hopefully crunching only cheese snacks in their wake.

A few other travelers joined us on board. There was the American dental anthropologist, transporting plaster molds of the jaws of indigenous tribal members he had collected in the jungle, as well as some Colombians who broke out a bottle of rum and passed it around to go along with the Cheez Doodles we had ripped open.

It was freezing in the unheated hold of the plane, but skimming just above the verdant Amazonian canopy, it didn't matter in the slightest. I was finally free of Brazil and on to Colombia.

Back in the Andes, Lefty and I would fling frisbees in a field full of cow pies sprouting psilocybe mushrooms, ride horses into the Magdalena River Valley, and stumble out of the jungle onto a Caribbean beach where three naked young women frolicked in the surf. (I don't think we were dreaming.)

After Colombia, Lefty headed south to Ecuador and I made my way north towards the States. My route took me to the Colombian island of San Andrés off the coast of Nicaragua. There I ended up sharing a dirt cheap room with a wild guy from Australia I'd met at the airport.

At some point, my new friend disappeared and returned to our room an hour later looking a little peaked. He threw about a dozen brightly-colored uninflated balloons, ends tied in a knot, onto the bed. They each contained two grams of cocaine he had swallowed that morning. They had just finished their journey through his digestive system intact, thankfully for him.

So here I was in a budget pension, the kind of place Colombian authorities regularly raided, with enough coke to park me in a dingy prison cell until middle age. It was a nervous, albeit high, few days before the home stretch of my travels.

I crossed the border back into the U.S. in Texas two years to the day

I had departed. As I hitchhiked my way across the country back to my parents in New Jersey, I had one final fright.

Somewhere in western Kentucky I got picked by a guy who very quickly confessed to being a hired killer returning from an assignment. Because I now knew his identity, I would also need to be dispatched, although no one would be paying for this hit. He said he had a .357 Magnum under his seat.

We drove on. The more time I spent with him, the more I came to believe this guy was full of shit. I also realized he was drunk. As the speedometer ticked towards 100 mph, I told him he had to let me out. I hadn't survived two years trekking around South America to end up squashed on the highway back in the States. Then, he would slow down to 9 mph. By the time he dropped me off, we were pals and I continued intact onto my childhood home.

NPR was not that far over the horizon.

# Chapter 23

# Benghazi

In 2011, I traveled to North Africa to cover the revolt against Muammar Gaddafi in the midst of the Arab Spring. NPR correspondent Peter Kenyon and I made our way overland from Cairo to Benghazi, the center of the rebel stronghold.

When we reached the city it seemed deceptively calm; but this was a highway war, with the front shifting constantly along the Mediterranean coastal road that stretched from Benghazi and beyond in the east to Tripoli, held by Gaddafi's army in the west. As Peter had pointed out, if government troops advanced on Benghazi and we were cut off from behind, we would be trapped. The fact that we'd entered the country through rebel-held territory meant that we had thrown our lot in with them, so we were technically in Libya illegally without visas.

It always seemed a little unfair over the years that I've missed out on lots of interesting stamps in my passport because I'm frequently entering countries with neither a functioning government nor customs official to greet me at the border. In the who's-got-the-fattest-passport competition, my documentation often appears pathetically slender.

Quite often as a journalist you get the sensation that you're headed the wrong way, passing people fleeing strife, mayhem, and earthquakes as you're heading towards disaster. In Libya, we would check the status of the front everyday like the weather forecast. If the conditions were favorable, we'd move as close to the fighting as was safe.

Peter is as calm a person as I've ever worked with in wartime. He'd direct our driver to precisely the point just beyond the reach of government rockets. If a mortar shell came in a bit too close, he'd suggest we back up a few hundred yards, never raising his voice. In tumultuous settings it can become pretty easy to kid yourself into thinking things are safer than they really are. All is fine, of course, until suddenly it isn't.

In Benghazi, we settled into a routine of going out daily and reporting the latest, coming back, and filing. Looking up at our high-rise hotel, you could tell immediately which rooms were occupied by the journalists, their satellite phone antennae sitting on the window ledges, all pointed in the exact same direction at the exact same angle, like soldiers in formation giving eyes right to their commander.

Every afternoon rebels and their supporters—definitely not in formation—would come marching down the road in front of the hotel setting off celebratory machine gun fire. Thousands of bullets shot into the air daily. It seemed that at some point some unlucky soul would be hapless enough to be standing where one of them returned to earth. We had to time our voice-tracking sessions to make sure they occurred on either side of the firearms display.

The story I tell again and again from this assignment was set in the Grecian ruins of Cyrene in Libya's Green Mountains, overlooking the sapphire Mediterranean. On the day we visited, picnicking Libyan families lounged among the ancient marble statues and columns.

At Cyrene, there were no guardrails, or even guards, for that matter, to shoo people away if they got too close to something precious. Kids could scramble around on the stones as they pleased. It was such a placid spot in a country beset by civil war.

The Libyans we talked to worried (correctly, it turns out) that their state would break apart further once the dictator fell. As we were leaving, we met Dr. Mayaar. He was an older gentleman missing most of his front teeth, but that didn't inhibit his broad smile in the least. Dr. Mayaar, who was kind of the caretaker at Cyrene, was an archaeologist. When we asked him how the ancient Greeks or Romans might have handled a tyrant like Gaddafi, his grin grew even wider. "They would have killed him," he said. "Immediately."

It's funny on assignment how you can become so well-acquainted with a place that just a few months earlier you had never even known existed. I mean Benghazi, Libya, definitely had not been on my vacation wish list. But pretty soon I knew where the best Turkish restaurant in town was, and I started to feel so at home that I began running, getting up early to jog along the waterfront road.

It was absolutely empty. Creepily empty. No people, no cars, just vacant buildings. I wondered at some point, Is this safe? Could somebody . . . I don't know . . . maybe kidnap me or something?

More than once I was woken out of my paranoid reverie by vicious barking. There was one mangy dog that waited for me in the exact same spot every day and would chase me until losing interest, maybe thirty yards down the road. After our first couple of encounters, I started running with a rock in each hand.

A few months after returning home from Libya, I read a piece in which a reporter told of running what sounded like more or less the same route I had—and getting shot at. Not so safe, I guess.

It was during this period that I got a bit friendly with Christopher Stevens. This was when he was the U.S. diplomatic representative in Benghazi, prior to his appointment as ambassador to Libya. We were staying at the same hotel and more than once had breakfast together. Not only was he an avid NPR listener, but we realized that we lived just a few blocks away from each other in D.C. As a career diplomat, though, he was hardly ever home. I told him his grass needed cutting.

Chris Stevens was one of those rare people you meet in life who are so exceptionally smart and accomplished and yet take a keen interest in hearing about what you're up to, what your opinion is. And it was clear he was deeply dedicated to his mission. That's what made it all the more horrifying when I learned that he had been killed when radicals attacked the U.S. Consulate in Benghazi in September of 2012. I think about Chris Stevens now and then when I jog past his house in the neighborhood.

# Chapter 24

# Return to Afghanistan

In some ways, my second trip to Afghanistan in 2014 with *Morning Edition* host Renée Montagne to cover the presidential election was more nerve-wracking than the first. Just prior to our visit, militants attacked the restaurant in the elegant and heavily-fortified Serena Hotel in Kabul, killing a well-known Afghan reporter, his family and five others. That same month a British-Swedish reporter was shot and killed on a Kabul street. And a few days after we arrived, a rogue Afghan police commander shot two journalists working for the Associated Press, killing one of them.

I was worried NPR might pull the plug on the entire trip, but we felt safe enough. Renée was on her tenth visit to Afghanistan and knew (and loved) the country well. We were also working with NPR's most talented and experienced photographer in conflict zones, David Gilkey.

Tragically, two years later David would be killed in a Taliban attack in Afghanistan along with NPR's Afghan interpreter, Zabihullah Tamanna. I never got to work with Zabi, but those who did spoke of his bravery, compassion and skill.

David was a force in the field, winning every news photography prize possible, often while putting himself at serious personal risk. But he was smart about the chances he took, and most of us relished the opportunity to be with him on assignment.

You'd be working on a story, and someone would look around and say, "Hey, where's Gilkey?" After a while, he'd turn up with a shit-eating grin and a memory card full of brilliant photographs that perfectly

Photo by David Gilkey at a presidential candidate rally, Bamiyan, Afghanistan, 2014

complemented the radio story you were working on. David and Zabi's deaths—the first and only ones NPR has ever suffered of reporters working in the field—reverberate around the organization to this day.

When we first arrived in Kabul, Renée and I were staying at the Gandamack Lodge, a guesthouse with a lovely garden popular with visiting reporters. Once we checked in, an employee showed us the safe room, a basement alcove with a heavy metal door we could slam shut in case of an attack. They also pointed out a ladder we could use to scale the wall surrounding the compound if we needed to escape. Our stay at the Gandamack was to be short-lived, though.

One day at Kabul airport, about to board a plane with one of the presidential candidates for a campaign stop in Bamiyan, my cell phone rang. It was the Gandamack. Government intelligence agents had shown up and were ordering the place to be closed. They had determined that the guest house was too ripe a Taliban target. We had 30 minutes to come pack up our stuff before the place was padlocked.

Thank goodness for our Kabul correspondent at the time, Sean Carberry. We gave him a pleading call, and he immediately mobilized his crew, who swooped into the Gandamack and gathered our gear. When we returned homeless from Bamiyan that night, we threw ourselves on the mercy of the folks at the Serena Hotel. They took pity on us and let us stay for a greatly discounted NPR-friendly rate. I still get holiday greeting emails from the place.

Security there was fortress-like. Once you made it past the concrete blast walls where your vehicle's undercarriage was checked for bombs with a mirror, you were personally searched, admitted through a steel door, then checked again, this time with a metal detector and X-ray for your gear. Guards then sent you through another steel door to the hotel lobby, where the last line of defense stood—a bunch of guys with AK-47s.

On election day the country was holding its collective breath. The Taliban had threatened to disrupt voting with attacks on polling stations, but that did not discourage the citizens. Thousands of Afghans in burkas and turbans, along with some in western clothes, lined up to cast their votes, risking their lives and thumbing their noses at the Taliban. It was a rare moment of exaltation in a country where day-to-day life can quickly turn from calm to catastrophe.

The other story on that trip that gave me some hope was a report I did on the Afghan Women's National Cycling Federation. I met the cyclists one day just outside Kabul during one of their training rides. These were fierce young women modestly dressed in long-sleeve jerseys and full-length tights, willing to absorb the jeers, hoots and occasional rocks thrown at them by men who feel Afghan females must keep a low profile.

The most talented among the group was a square-jawed rider in wraparound sunglasses named Marjan Sadeqi, who the year before had spent five days in the hospital after she'd been purposely rammed

Marjan Sadeqi and her Afghan women
cyclist teammates, Kabul 2014

by a motorbike and knocked unconscious. During a break she told me, "I'm not the kind of woman to be scared. When I make up my mind to do something, I do it. So once I recovered, I got back on my bike, and here I am cycling again."

Unfortunately, since the takeover of the Taliban in August 2021, riding in Afghanistan has ceased for these young women, and members of the team have been forced to flee the country.

# Chapter 25

# Embedding

My third trip to Afghanistan was in the fall of 2017, and this time I embedded with the U.S. military, first with the Army and then the Marines. This would be NPR's initial return to the country after the tragedy of David Gilkey and Zabihullah Tamanna, so the company was being extremely cautious.

I would be going with NPR's Pentagon correspondent Tom Bowman, who had been in another vehicle and survived the attack that killed David and Zabi. Our bosses told us that under no circumstances were we to accompany patrols "outside the wire," meaning into enemy-controlled territory, and there would be positively no embedding with the Afghan military, whose skill level could be spotty at best.

This was fine with me although I knew Tom, who in many ways is as tough as any soldier, was itching to get right back into the thick of things.

Tom and I arrived in Kabul after a 14-hour flight and headed for our safe house. Instead of the beautiful Serena Hotel or cozy, now shuttered, Gandamack Lodge, this time we would be staying at a purposely nondescript place down a rutted road.

The house manager told us, there was no way the Taliban would ever think to attack this spot unless they were specifically targeting someone. As usual, if needed, there was a secure room fortified with an iron door and stocked with enough food and water to hold us until any Taliban siege ended.

Before heading out, NPR had outfitted us with combat gear. While I have traveled with a Kevlar vest and a helmet on a number of occasions, they have often sat in the trunk of the car, too heavy and hot to put on unless things appeared to be going seriously south. However, when embedding with the Army and the Marines, if they tell you to put on your body armor, you better or you're not going anywhere with them. What's more, just in case there's an incident, front and center on your vest and on the back of your helmet is a little patch or piece of duct tape indicating your blood type (AB positive for me).

Instantly adding 15 pounds to your body weight takes some getting used to. When you try to stand up from a chair, it feels like you've left your seatbelt fastened. Looking down from the top of a stairway, you need to steady yourself to avoid an Inspector Clouseau nosedive. It probably didn't help that the weekend before departing for Kabul a friend and I had gone mountain biking with a pro rider, which left my back in spasms.

On one shoulder of your vest is an emergency ripcord. It's pulled when you have to shed your Kevlar instantly, like when a medic needs to get to your sucking chest wound pronto. It bypasses the elaborate Velcro system that binds the vest to you, so that everything quickly peels away.

One day in Helmand Province, we were out with the Marines at an FOB, a forward operating base. This was the heart of Taliban country so, of course, body armor was mandatory. As I was gearing up for our departure from the base, I got discombobulated and accidentally tugged my ripcord. In a slow-motion striptease, huge sections of my vest began to fall away from me.

At first, I was totally confused, as belts, fabric and Kevlar plates started sloughing off in my hands. Then I quickly became mortified. The battle-hardened warriors surrounding me, who I had truly come to admire for their courage, humanity and smarts, tried not to giggle. As if this were not enough, I also managed to break the strap on my helmet, so it sat cockeyed on my head, giving me quite the doofus look. The Marines took pity, fixed my headgear, and I reassembled my vest.

As it turned out, it was not a bad idea that I was wearing body armor on that return trip from the FOB. At one point, as our Chinook heli-

With reporter Tom Bowman and our military escorts at Camp Shorab
Marine base, Helmand Province, Afghanistan, 2017

copter made its way over the flat dusty terrain back to the main base at
Camp Shorab, I felt a bump and heard what sounded to me like landing gear lowering. Immediately the armed Marine manning the wide-
open rear section of our helicopter was on high alert, and I saw flares
shooting out the back of the aircraft. Then there was the slight smell
of gasoline.

As I was to discover a bit later on, we had likely been hit by some
small arms fire, probably Taliban pot shots, which nicked a fuel line.

Those red-hot decoy flares shooting out were meant to draw the aim of heat seeking missiles, if any headed our way.

The only harm I would suffer from rockets on this trip was from friendly fire. It was our last night in Helmand, and just before midnight Tom and I went to record some outgoing illumination mortars the troops fired a couple of times a week just to remind the Taliban, "Hey, we're here. Don't forget."

We were instructed to wear helmet, vest, ear protection and eye protection. As these mortars were outgoing, I figured they would sound kind of like a whoosh. I didn't have the slightest inkling as to how monstrously loud these things were, so I set myself up pretty close by with my recorder, microphone and some crappy little sponge earplugs. Thank goodness, I was not wearing my headphones, which would have amplified the blast in my ears.

When the first mortar went off, I felt a slam to my forehead and saw bright stars, like in a cartoon when the Road Runner drops an anvil on Wile E. Coyote's noggin. Immediately I knew I was in trouble, as my ears felt like I was underwater.

When I woke up the next morning with the same sensation, I realized this problem would not be passing soon. In the end, I lost approximately 20 percent of my hearing; so today I wear hearing aids. At least I can say, "No, I'm not losing my hearing because I'm an old fart. Nope, I lost it when I was in the shit (dramatic pause here) in Afghanistan."

As on earlier visits to Afghanistan, this time too I looked for a story of people trying to make the best of a bad situation. I found it with the Miraculous Love Kids Music School.

We met them in the garden of a heavily-guarded guesthouse. A group of young teenage girls, all headscarves and concentration, were stretching tentative fingers across their guitar strings. Looking on was their instructor and school founder, 56-year-old Lanny Cordola from Los Angeles. He had his own head covering, a green bandana, holding in check a graying ponytail that drifted down his back.

This former arena rocker, who has played guitar with Guns N' Roses and the Beach Boys, was now devoting himself to teaching music to Kabul's street kids. Cordola had been moving between L.A. and Kabul for the past three years, toting donated guitars and a desire to turn around some young lives.

Cordola's musical mission began in 2012, when he read an article about two sisters who had been killed in Kabul. The girls had been selling trinkets on the street with their little sister Mursal. As two of the girls went in one direction, Mursal headed a different way. A suicide bomber struck, killing the two older girls.

Two years later Cordola tracked down Mursal (like many people in Afghanistan she went by just one name) and her family in Kabul. He found them living in poverty.

"I had no idea it was going to turn into this thing that we're doing now," Cordola told me. "And when I brought a guitar on one of the visits, [Mursal] wanted to learn. And so I just kept coming back, and eventually they started bringing more friends, and we would drive around and we'd see all these girls on the streets."

Thus was born Kabul's Miraculous Love Kids Music School. The group now had close to 60 members, mostly girls, ranging in age from six to sixteen.

With her acoustic guitar perched on her lap, Mursal, now 13, settled into a sofa. She was a star pupil, dressed in a scarlet headscarf, pink shirt and denim vest. Mursal positively sparkled with a broad, dimply grin.

It was highly unusual for young women to be playing rock 'n' roll in Afghanistan, especially in public. Nevertheless, Cordola said he met with very little resistance from the families, in part because his foundation was paying for schooling for many of these kids.

Sixteen-year-old Madina Mohammadi, the other guitar star of the class and a former street kid, had never attended school before teaming up with Cordola. She said she was learning English—plus some other things. "Mr. Lanny tell me something good about life, and guitar teach me a little bit too about life," she said, "about feeling."

Lanny Cordola and The Miraculous Love Kids, Kabul, 2017

Through Cordola, the Beach Boys' Brian Wilson took an interest in the group and invited Mursal to visit him in the U.S. It's too bad her visa was denied. Wilson did send over voice and music tracks for his song *Love and Mercy* that the girls mixed with their own performing. To hear Mursal's sweet voice intertwining with Brian Wilson's, knowing all she has been through, still sends a shiver every time I hear it.

Since the Taliban takeover students and families of The Miraculous Love Kids Music School have had to flee their country to Pakistan. The good news is that they are safe there and learning new songs.

# Chapter 26

# Ebola

Covering the 2014 Ebola crisis in Africa was a very different kind of assignment. In hostile environments, the danger you need to avoid is usually visible or at least physical—a minefield, a mob, a treacherous road, an interviewee with smoke coming out of his ears. This is not the case with a highly contagious virus that causes internal bleeding and is frequently fatal.

NPR had a very specific protocol we were supposed to follow when traveling into the hot zone: Do not enter a hospital ward with actively ill patients, constantly wash your hands and absolutely no touching another human.

What an odd experience it was to go a couple of weeks with no physical contact with another person. When you were introduced to someone, you just kind of nodded; and then, if you ran into them afterwards, you might tap clothed elbows. (These, of course, are practices that came into much more common use once the coronavirus pandemic was upon us.)

NPR gave us a long list of products to pack to keep us healthy, which we stocked up on before departing: face masks, latex gloves, hand sanitizers, chlorine wipes, rubber boots, first-aid kit. I was traveling with Anders Kelto, one of our newest science reporters at the time, and all the hygiene products were stuffed into one of his bags.

Unfortunately, that suitcase didn't make it to the capital, Freetown, until about three hours before our return flight back to the U.S. And so during our stay, we made do with the couple of bottles of hand sanitizer and some wipes we found in a market our first day there.

Even if you never lose a suitcase, precarious assignments where you're filing on deadline can be tremendously stressful. The electricity is sketchy, there's no time to eat, and the clock seems to be constantly ticking down to zero hour—filing time.

The producer and reporter are usually working shoulder to shoulder on their laptops or in adjacent hotel rooms, with the producer pulling tape cuts and mapping out a structure for the piece as the reporter writes the script and fine tunes what the producer has given them.

Once they're done with the script, they send it to Washington and then call in for an edit, with the producer playing the tape cuts over the speaker for the D.C. editor as the reporter reads the copy. The editor times the story, points out what worked and what didn't and suggests trims if the piece is longer than the show you're filing for has budgeted.

Then it's time to record the reporter's voice tracks. Shut the windows, turn off the ceiling fan, and hopefully the room is quiet enough. Sometimes I may throw a towel over the reporter's head as they read the script in order to make the room sound less hollow.

When we were in Freetown, our hotel was not far from the beach; so we thought it would be a nice effect to record Ander's voice during interviews with the host in Washington on the balcony, with the gentle splashing of the ocean in the background. *Morning Edition* seemed to like the technique, while a producer for *All Things Considered* thought we were standing in front of an air conditioning vent.

Next, you need to upload the audio to D.C., which requires a clear signal from your sat phone to the satellite. (Remember my Two Stooges escapade with Scott Simon in Baghdad?) This wasn't an issue most of the time, but one day out in the Sierra Leone countryside filing on a drizzly morning, the cloud cover was impeding communication from my hotel room, so I went out into a muddy parking lot. With my fixer holding an umbrella over me, I took out my compass, aimed the sat phone antenna and made my deadline.

One day we decided to follow an Ebola case from the time it was first reported until the patient was admitted to a clinic. For the first time in my career, I found myself being a literal ambulance chaser as

Trying to hit the satellite and make my deadline,
Bo, Sierra Leone, 2014

we trailed behind a screaming siren to an outlying village. There, on a porch, health workers in white moon suits and masks found a slouching teenager complaining of a headache. Without ever laying a latex gloved hand on him, they nudged him into the ambulance, kicking the rear door closed.

We then tailed along again as they drove to a facility on a military base, where the soldiers didn't seem to be expecting them and took particular exception to my microphone. After a few tense minutes, the young man was led into a huge outdoor tent and placed in a bed alongside other infected people.

Later at our hotel, listening back to the tape as we worked on our story, I realized that the name of the kid didn't match the name that

Roadside temperature check, Sierra Leone, 2014

the dispatcher had given to the ambulance driver. Slowly Anders and I came to the uncomfortable realization that the driver had likely picked up the wrong person and that a boy with perhaps just an everyday headache had been mistaken for a symptomatic Ebola victim. Now he was confined to a crowded facility with highly infectious patients.

Our story went from a tale of how the system was efficiently working to one of incompetence. The woman managing the NGO that oversaw the dispatching system tearfully begged us not to report the snafu. We apologized to her but said we were obligated to give our listeners the complete story. Happily, when we checked on our young patient just before leaving the country, we were told he had tested negative for Ebola.

Things felt even more acute when we traveled into the interior of Sierra Leone to the town of Kenema, ground zero for the outbreak. Along the way we passed through quarantine villages where residents were not allowed to leave and vehicles passing through could not stop. There were periodic roadside checkpoints where blue gowned health workers aimed pistol-like thermometers at us. A high fever is the first symptom of Ebola and most people are not infectious until they run a temperature. Anders and I dutifully made sure to check ours twice a day.

At the ward in Kenema, we met an Ebola survivor named Dauda Fullah. Those who live through the disease are likely immune from reinfection. The 23-year-old had worked as a lab technician before the epidemic, now he was drawing blood from patients in the same hospital where he had been treated and where every member of his family had died from the virus. He offered hope to those infected, telling them, "Look, I've been through this, and I survived. Just do what the doctors say and keep fighting."

We met others who were still recovering and perhaps remained infectious. They were isolated behind white plastic sheeting and I had to put my microphone on a telescoping fish pole to record them from eight feet away. People monitoring us made sure my mic cable never brushed against the plastic and if the bottom of the fish pole touched the ground they told me to spray it with chlorine wash, just like we did with our boots when leaving the contamination area. The virus could not last long outside of a host, but if you came in contact with it during that brief interim, you could get sick.

And then there was 3-year-old Ibrahim. He had been brought in with his mother and two older brothers, everyone deathly ill. Ibrahim and his siblings survived. Their mother did not. Now he wanted to marry the nurse who helped bring him back to health at the Kenema Hospital. She teasingly told us she'd accepted his proposal.

On these high stress assignments, you want to travel with someone you know has your back and with whom you are simpatico. It's especially gratifying to collaborate with a reporter who is not only talented and works hard but, once you've filed your story, also enjoys having a beer and cracking jokes. Anders was all of these. I have to say I have been blessed; by and large, my NPR trips have been remarkably ass-hole-free.

We stayed in the nearby city of Bo while doing our Kenema report-ing. Our hotel was a gloomy place with flickering fluorescent lighting that gave everything a blue hue. Anders' suitcase may not have made it to Sierra Leone but his little traveling guitar did, although with only the top two strings intact.

At the end of a long, fairly depressing day, we sat around under the buzzing hazy light in Bo composing *The Talkin' Ebola Blues*, Anders on E and A strings and me on harmonica. Lamentably, the session was never recorded, so it remains just a fable in Sierra Leone, like a lost Beatles track.

Back in the capital, Freetown, on the evening before our departure home, I stumbled upon a scene I just had to document. Shops and restaurants along the beachfront had been shuttered because of the Ebola emergency, but on this night at least one place was open. It was an outdoor fitness club, a kind of Muscle Beach Freetown.

In the sand under the palm trees sat thick rusted barbells and a crude wooden bench press. Four pairs of breathless young women were run-ning through what looked like self-defense drills. It turns out they were rehearsing for an anti-drug movie called *Gunshot*. One of the actors was a petite 22-year-old named Frances Nicole. She told me she would love it if her fight scenes led to a starring role in the film. Even in Sierra Leone, in the midst of a devastating epidemic, a young actor could still hope for her big break.

Once we were back in the States everyone kept their distance, even my wife. For 10 days, Anders and I continued to take our temperatures morning and evening to make sure we weren't incubating the virus. For my first time ever at NPR after returning from a tough assignment, my boss suggested I take some time off. You're not quarantined, he assured me, just . . . don't come in the office, okay?

Looking back at Ebola from the calamity that is Covid-19, that ear-lier experience now seems so much less dire.

# Chapter 27

# Absurdities . . .

Shenanigans abound in the field. My hall-of-fame entry didn't occur on NPR's dime, but rather during a leave I took for a broadcast journalism fellowship at the University of Chicago. It was a fantastic getaway from the news grind, with a year of taking courses, attending seminars and exploring South Side blues joints. The fellowship ended with a trip to Moscow, Latvia, and Uzbekistan; it was at this last stop where turmoil found me.

We were in Samarkand, the ancient city on the Silk Road. I was traveling with a crew of journalists including two other NPR reporters— Jacki Lyden (the party animal from Chapter 16) and our South Africa correspondent at the time, John Matisonn.

One evening we went to visit the spectacular 15th-century Bibi Khanym mosque, with its monumental turquoise dome. Around 11 p.m. as we were getting ready to head back to our hotel, a large wedding party came marching down the road. The bride and groom drove by slowly in a car, followed by a horde of singing, dancing, drinking men on foot. It seemed a little off that these Muslims were consuming alcohol, but Middle East veteran Jacki said, "Let's follow them. I know Muslims. It'll be fine. It'll be fun."

Jacki, John, our friend Patsy from CBS, and I broke away from our main group and joined the celebration winding down the road. At some point, though, the bride and groom peeled off, and we found ourselves on a darkened side street with a couple of dozen drunk revelers. This was soon after the fall of Communism, and these Uzbeks were making the most of their newly found freedom.

Then it was time to dance. The men formed a large circle, clapping and singing; and one of them grabbed me by the arm to join in. I immediately could feel by his grip that I had no choice in the matter and that things might be taking a bad turn. But I figured I would play along, and then we could get the hell out of there.

Once the dance ended, I hustled back to my friends and told them what was up and that we needed to leave. But then my dance partner returned, grabbed me by the shirt, and insisted otherwise. I announced I was going to break free and that we should all run for it.

I slapped his hand away, which half ripped off my shirt, and sprinted. He gave chase but then quickly gave up. When I turned around, I saw that for some reason my friends hadn't taken off; and when the thug returned, he grabbed Patsy by the arm. Edging closer, I tried to persuade him to let go of her, but he was using her as bait to lure me back.

By this point, Jacki had had enough; she kicked the brute in the nuts. He released Patsy but not before punching her in the stomach. We all madly scrambled away.

Safely back on the main road, we regrouped and assessed. I had pulled my calf muscle sprinting, and the thugs had stolen my wallet from my back pocket. Far worse, Patsy tearfully revealed to us that she was pregnant. We were horrified, fearing the damage from the punch. Thank goodness, months later Patsy would give birth to a very healthy boy.

The next morning our interpreter took us to the neighborhood police precinct to report the incident and see if we could retrieve my wallet. As we drove there, we realized the station was exactly adjacent to the spot where the assault had taken place. Had the cops looked out the window, they could have seen the whole thing.

Inside, the station was a free-for-all. No one was in uniform. It was impossible to tell who were the cops and who were the criminals. People were speaking Russian, Uzbek and Tadjik. Our interpreter tried to make sense of it all.

Once we found the official in charge, we gave him a detailed description of the tough guy—mid-20's, black hair, fit. The chief assured us there couldn't have been very many weddings in Samarkand that night and that he would find our tormentor.

As far as my wallet was concerned, he said that someone had probably picked it up on the street and tossed it into a mailbox. Happens all the time, he told me. It would definitely be waiting for me at the U.S. Embassy in Moscow when I returned there for our final stop, complete with credit cards and driver's license. Nobody wanted them, just the cash. Sure.

He told us he would send some officers to our hotel at the end of the day to take us to the city's main police station, where I could ID the perp. It was a huge embarrassment to these officials that American journalists had been attacked while visiting their recently liberated country.

That evening a police vehicle did come by to pick us up, but when I opened the rear door to get into the car, the door came off its hinges, with me holding it in my hand. Reattaching the thing as best I could, I jammed it in place for the drive downtown. This was not the NYPD.

At this station, things did seem a bit more organized than the first precinct, and officers were even wearing actual uniforms. The lead inspector informed me that they had indeed apprehended my assailant.

We were standing in a hallway, and he told me that he was going to open a door; in that room would be the drunken bully. I merely had to ID him. He then dramatically swung open the door; there slumped in a chair was a dissipated-looking man in his fifties with graying hair who glanced up at me with very sad eyes. Is there any need to mention that my wallet never turned up in Moscow?

# . . . and Embarrassments

Of course, there has been plenty of nonsense on the road with Scott Simon—like the time we somehow persuaded NPR to send us to Hawaii. On this trip I had a big wave rider give Scott a surfing lesson. We attached a wireless mic to Scott and sent him into the waves. As he bobbed up and down 100 yards offshore, my sound technician, Manoli Wetherell, and I quickly realized that the transmitter belted to Scott's waist was cutting in and out as it went under the water. We waved excitedly to Scott, but he merely waved back, thinking we were just being friendly. I worked around the sound dropouts to produce the piece.

The ostensibly serious reason for our island excursion was to report on the emerging Hawaiian independence movement. But let's be honest here, Scott and I just wanted to get to Hawaii. One breezy day we found ourselves on the breathtaking island of Kauai interviewing one of the local independence leaders.

We drove up a long driveway on a verdant hillside and talked to the big bearded man outside his rustic cabin. Things quickly turned odd, however, when the guy started telling us about astrally projecting himself back to his days fighting in the Vietnam War. From there the discussion only became more disjointed. At some point Scott passed me a note. This guy is nuts, it read.

We tried to wrap things up but not before our host played us a little something on the long bamboo instrument sitting beside him, his nose flute. When he finished, we clapped politely; and Scott for some reason asked, "How long have you been playing the piano?" At that point I had to excuse myself.

Sometimes you have to do some things that you're not particularly proud of to get the story. That's what happened when Scott and I were reporting from Ponce, Puerto Rico.

In 1937, local police fired on citizens during a protest there, and we found out that the town museum had a video explaining the story. We thought we might be able to use some of the audio from the film in our piece. The museum curator was excited to set us up in a screening room, but as we sat watching, we quickly realized that this was a two-hour saga about the entire history of Puerto Rico. We were pressed for time and, well, the words just came out of my mouth, "Can you fast forward to the massacre, please?"

The career moment of which I am most ashamed occurred on a trip to Ecuador. Science reporter John Nielsen and I were reporting on the globalization of shrimp farming and production. Near the coastal town of Muisne we found the most gripping part of the story.

Traveling with a woman from Greenpeace, who was smartly dressed in a crisp white shirt, we motored by outboard canoe into a swampy region. In tall rubber boots we then tramped into the jungle, which required negotiating a few slippery downed logs. Regrettably, our Greenpeace friend lost her balance and with an arms-windmilling "whoa, whoa, whoa" she plopped into the muck. I don't think that white blouse would ever be the same again.

After more trudging, we reached a spot in the mangrove swamp where two women were digging deep into that muck by hand for some small crabs and shellfish that they could sell for a tiny income. The area was hot and mosquito-infested. To try to fend off the bugs, the women burned a few twigs in a small aluminum pot, creating just a bit of smoke that they waved around. Meanwhile, we were fully lathered up in bug repellent. My heart went out to them.

I followed the women around with my microphone as they dug, trying not to repeat the Greenpeace wardrobe malfunction. They quietly unfolded a very moving story for us, a tale of lives of endless hardship trying to eke out a living. And then, just as we were finishing up, my digital recorder somehow slipped out of my hand and into the muck.

It was a god-awful moment. I immediately reached down and yanked my machine out of the mud. But when I wiped it off and turned it on, it would not play. I had no idea if the audio was permanently lost or if technicians back in Washington might be able to restore it.

What ensued was the least professional moment of an already very tarnished résumé. I unleashed a screaming, ranting, teeth gnashing, profanity laced tirade in front of the two poor Ecuadorians, who were now cowering in the foliage, fearing that the crazy American might actually physically explode. Later John, harkening back to *King Lear*, called the fit my Breslow-on-the-Heath moment.

As I was trying to recover my composure, John hiked back to our canoe, retrieved my backup machine, and we redid the entire sequence with the women. Of course, as is frequently the case with a redo, it wasn't nearly as powerful as the first take. The good news is that back in Washington our techs were able to retrieve the original audio, and we put together a compelling piece. The bad news is that I likely entered local lore in Muisne, Ecuador, as the journalist who came to town and completely lost his mind in the jungle.

I will admit to a bit more humiliation, this time again with reporter John Nielson. We were on a trip to Alaska for a report on the 10th anniversary of the Exxon Valdez oil spill in Prince William Sound, which took us to the beautiful village of Cordova. We went there to inspect beaches where oil still lurked just below the pebbly surface. As we were stepping onto a seaplane for a short flight to an oily spot, our guides asked, "Where are your boots?" Ah . . . what boots?

We city slickers didn't realize that when you travel by seaplane, you don't just pull up on the beach. You dock 10 or 20 icy, knee-deep feet from shore, so once we landed at our isolated cove we were in an awkward predicament. Luckily, our hosts in their waders, were very hospitable.

When we asked, "What do we do now?", they shrugged and said, "Hop on", and offered the two of us piggyback rides from the plane to the beach. Even the terns and cormorants of Prince William Sound could sense the indignity.

We were also reporting on the Alaska oil pipeline during that trip. As part of the story, I traveled solo above the Arctic Circle to Arctic Village, a tiny outpost of about 185 mainly indigenous Gwich'in people. I was there to catch the end of the fall migration of the Porcupine caribou, during which close to 200,000 of the animals make their way south across the region. As they pass by Arctic Village, subsistence hunters shoot them for food. We wanted to find out from villagers if the infrastructure of the pipeline was affecting the animals' movements.

I took a small plane from Fairbanks and touched down on a simple landing strip. When I hopped out and met my local contact, she greeted me with a familiar sounding question, "Where's your food?" Ah . . . what food? The place didn't have much in the way of groceries or restaurants. I was 0 for 2 in Alaskan etiquette.

I did track down a can of Dinty Moore Beef Stew that sustained me for a day or two. A slab of caribou meat on the side sure would have been nice.

I managed one other major blunder in Alaska, but this one happened while on my very first vacation with my future wife, Jessica. The trip began with an auspicious moment in the town of Sitka. We'd arrived there during salmon spawning season, and the water was bubbling with the fish.

One day we went out on a small boat with the manager for the local public radio station. As we tooled around, a big ol' salmon jumped right into the boat, flipping and flapping around at our feet. I figured this must be a common spawning-season phenomena, but our host told us that in more than 30 years living in Alaska this was the first time it had ever happened to him—or anyone he knew. For the rest of our Sitka visit, whenever we were introduced to people, they would say, "Oh you're the NPR folks. I hear you had a salmon jump in your boat." Turns out our inconceivable fish story did not portend much positive for the rest of the trip.

Disgrace arrived full on a week later during a sea-kayaking excursion up Glacier Bay. An outfitter dropped us off, with instructions to pick us up at that put-in spot four days later.

That first day was magnificent, with orcas and sea lions frolicking alongside our double-person kayak. Eagles glided above, as common as starlings. With the sun setting, we hauled to shore, cooked dinner and made sure to store our provisions in Grizzly-bear-proof containers a good 50 yards from our tent.

There was something odd about that sunset, though. Sure, it was golden and stunning, but according to my compass it was going down in the east. Huh? Is there something about the sunset so far north in Alaska in the summertime? Could it somehow appear to happen in the east? It's amazing what you can convince yourself of when there's no GPS.

By the second day, it was becoming clear that, somehow, we were lost—perhaps going in the wrong direction. But what could we do except keep on paddling? There was absolutely no one around to ask, and these were pre-cell phone days. Also, we started noticing whirlpools appearing in the water. What could this mean?

In the afternoon of Day 2, we spotted a fishing boat stopped in the distance. Paddling with wild desperation, we finally pulled up alongside it and explained ourselves to the fisherman. He laughed, pulled out a map, and said, "You guys are almost back to town. Just make sure you stay to the right up ahead. You're lucky, if you had kept going straight, you would have entered the open sea, which would have been trouble." That's why we were seeing whirlpools.

Once we were back, I realized I needed to go tell our outfitter that he didn't have to pick us up at the rendezvous point. With my tail between my legs, I reported what I figured most likely had happened. When he dropped us off, the clouds were so leaden and low that we must have immediately got turned around and headed south instead of north. I said, "Guess this must happen to kayakers all the time." To which the boat captain explained that in all his decades of sending off boaters, this was the very first time this had ever occurred.

The topper was that because of our wayward route, not only were we paddling against the tides the whole time, which could swell by as much as 25-feet, but we had camped in the red zone on the map—the area with a large Grizzly population, to be avoided at all cost.

Here I was the Eagle Scout, the Mt. Everest veteran, who had screwed up so royally on our first adventure together. And yet, Jessica married me anyway.

# Chapter 29

# Robin Williams, Steve Jobs and the Prince of Puke

Working with NPR colleagues in the field is often a highlight of my job, but it is refreshing when you get to team up with an outside person. They can bring an unexpected sensibility that shakes up that story-telling style with which you're so comfortable.

Over the decades I've had the opportunity to collaborate with authors, musicians, filmmakers, adventurers, comedians and other journalists on everything from reports about the brothels of Budapest and the Cu Chi tunnels of Vietnam to stories about jokes from ancient Greece and documentaries on the classic novels *To Kill a Mockingbird* and *The Grapes of Wrath*.

I produced those last two pieces with writer David Sheff, a fabulous journalist who has become a great friend. He's probably best known for his book, *Beautiful Boy*, about his son Nic's terrible meth addiction. Thankfully, Nic, who as a little kid accompanied David and me on a couple of our reporting trips, survived and is thriving. *Beautiful Boy* was turned into a film starring Timothée Chalamet and Steve Carell.

Now and then in this profession you get to brush up against famous folks, and it was through David that I had a couple of unlikely celebrity encounters, including a quirky conversation with Steve Jobs. David's brother was Job's cook at the time and lived in an out building at the late Apple titan's Palo Alto estate. This was a bit before he had become all caps STEVE JOBS, but he was already a major player at the time.

One evening, as we were sitting around having dinner, Steve wandered in looking flummoxed. It seems he was headed to New York the next day for a blind date and was hoping for a little first-meet-up advice. We assured him he'd do just fine and I'm almost certain that our pep talk helped speed the introduction of the iPhone a few years later.

My other namedrop-worthy moment around this time was with the late actor and comedian Robin Williams. Young Nic Sheff was friends with Robin Williams' son and when I was in San Francisco working with David, we were all invited to Robin's house for a kids birthday party. In the backyard I got to schmooze and eat cake with the comedian, and we all made plans to go out to dinner together that night.

I arrived first at some trendy San Francisco eatery and was told that the place was absolutely completely booked well into the next century. Then I mentioned I was meeting Robin Williams and his wife. Instantly a waiter lifted a table out from the back, scootched over some other patrons, threw on a tablecloth and—voilà—Williams party of four, this way please.

The most entertaining collaborations of my career had to be the stories I worked on with filmmaker John Waters. The notorious director of *Pink Flamingos*, *Multiple Maniacs* and *Hairspray* first accompanied me to Bengies Drive-In outside of Baltimore to do a piece about one of the area's last outdoor screens. John was in his element, a throwback place that opened in 1956, not far from his beloved Charm City.

I knew that my time with the busy director would be limited; and I would never be able to get him to sit down, write a script, and then come into a studio to record his narration. I decided these would be non-scripted stories in which I would ask John questions and then string together his answers, which often included his own drive-in remembrances of the B-movies that helped inspire his gloriously decadent oeuvre.

He told about being a little kid and watching forbidden films in the spirt of *I Dismember Mama* and *I Spit on Your Grave* through binoculars from a nearby hilltop. He was a fearless interviewer, walking around the theater lot and tapping on car windows to ask patrons, among other things, if they'd ever been caught in flagrante delicto in their cars at the drive-in.

Our next story was about a demolition derby in which we anchored a tape machine to the dashboard of a car that was doomed to be clobbered. Once again, John exuded love of the subject matter. He recalled being a child obsessed with car crashes, smashing his little toy cars with a hammer and telling his parents, "Look, there's been a terrible accident." He even revealed how his mom and dad would bring him to the junkyard to show him the totaled aftermath of real car wrecks.

It certainly didn't hurt our story that we had the sound of colliding fenders, screeching tires and a delirious crowd to mix in. Over the course of the evening, we saw at least a dozen cars get pulverized. If you're keeping score at home, the winner was a 1972 Buick LeSabre.

The great side benefit from working with John Waters is that every holiday season over the years I get one of his Christmas cards. One December it was a photo of a Christmas tree going up in flames as John, nattily attired in a tuxedo, glances over incredulously from his easy chair. Another year, I received a card showcasing some sort of mutant. But my all-time treasured gift from the director was a clear plastic Christmas-tree bulb embossed with *Seasons Greetings*, featuring a giant rubber cockroach staring out.

Years later I got to chat briefly with John when we were interviewing him for his latest book. He was up in New York, so I spoke to him down the audio hookup line and said, "You probably don't remember me, but we once did some stories together." I mentioned the demolition derby. To this John lit up, "Of course I remember. Actually, that demolition derby story inspired one of my intimate scenes. In it I'm having sex in a car as it's getting crashed into." What an unexpected career highlight. I helped spark an X-rated scene for the Pope of Trash, the Prince of Puke. I will put that on the shelf alongside my Peabody Awards any day.

# Chapter 30

# Way Outdoors

Something from my Boy Scout days at Camp NoBeBoSco—beyond our scoutmaster's self-abuse instructions—must have stuck, because I have been pitching outdoor adventure stories at NPR from day one.

Over the years I have successfully lobbied my executive producers to send me to Yosemite to report on rock climbers, to New England to cover mountain biking races, and to Colorado to talk to bicycle-riding Olympians. On that Rockies trip I began experimenting with the best way to record while biking.

This first attempt was slapstick, even by Breslow standards. I wanted to tape myself riding the paved road up Boulder's famed Flagstaff Mountain with an elite cyclist. I didn't have wireless mics with me at the time, so I clipped a lapel mic on the guy I was taping and ran the cord over to the cassette deck I had draped around my neck.

We rode up the 7,000-foot peak side-by-side, keeping close so that the mic wire wouldn't pull out. This required some balancing. Any time I wanted to ask a question I would lean over and shout towards the mic. The technique worked pretty well, although the drivers behind us were having conniptions.

On another occasion, I cajoled women's downhill mountain biking champion Cindy Whitehead to take me down the Kamikaze run at Mammoth Mountain ski resort in California. It was an early June day and one of the ski trails still had some snow, so as we rode up the chairlift with our bikes strapped to the back of the chair, we were accompanied by a few skiers heading for their final runs of the season.

Kamikaze was a loose gravelly route free of snow, on which we would be hitting 40 miles-an-hour. I hired a sound technician from San Francisco to do the recording, which would allow me to concentrate on not wiping out. When he showed up with a shotgun mic the size of a bazooka, with the thinnest of spongy windscreens on the tip, I knew I was in trouble.

"You're not really going to use that, are you?" I asked him. "You'll get nothing but wind noise."

"Don't worry," he told me. "I know what I'm doing."

At the end of the day, the tape, as expected, was unusable. I sent the tech packing back to San Francisco and recorded Cindy on my own the following morning, strapping my tape machine to my chest with duct tape and using a lapel mic. I got the skidding action audio I needed and managed to stay upright on the bike.

Not all my sports stories have taken place way outdoors. One day I found myself in a speedo and goggles at a local college swimming pool profiling the Beltway Bottom Feeders. Surprisingly, this wasn't a club of politicians or lobbyists. It was an underwater hockey team. Men and women wearing snorkels and masks, carrying tiny 12-inch mini-hockey sticks. Their recruiting poster said it all: *You Must be Kidding!* Well, they were; but then again, they weren't.

At a practice scrimmage, someone shouted, "Sticks up, go!" and a dozen flippered swimmers dove down eight feet aiming towards a weighted puck. As team founder and animated underwater true believer, Dave Sun, told me, "Underwater hockey is a horrible spectator sport. From the surface, it looks like a trout farm."

Unlike ice hockey, water is a great equalizer, so men and women match up pretty well. Guys on the team got dreamy-eyed when they told me about one of the Bottom Feeders' all-time all-stars, a synchronized swimmer who could hold her breath like a sea lion.

The longer you can stifle your breathing, the greater skill you will have in this sport. Dave Sun pointed out, "If you're comfortable feeling like you're about to run out of air and suffocate, if that doesn't freak you out, that makes you a good underwater hockey player."

As your lungs are bursting, it becomes a matter of will power. How

Riding the Rio Grande through the Taos Box with sound engineer Suraya Mohamed,
a river guide and reporter John Burnett (partially obscured), 1993

badly do you want to make that goal—enough that you're willing to
lose some brain cells?

Eight feet down you can't yell, "Hey I'm open, pass it to me." Instead,
you tap on the floor of the pool with your stick. Our hydrophones captured the underwater knocking sound.

I found the competition withering, a feeding frenzy down there. People looked like human catfish dragging along the bottom, thrashing
and spinning and trying for the puck, pushing and passing and tapping. All the while I remained mostly suspended perpendicular above
the fray, bobbing back up for a desperate gulp of air before ever getting anywhere near the action.

Rebounded from the oxygen deficit, I dove back down, and this time
I actually touched the puck. All of a sudden, there was no one between
me and the goal. But my timing was completely off. I was utterly out of

air and had to wildly swim to the surface, leaving the puck and some gray matter behind—a classic rookie mistake.

At the end of the evening, the competitors dragged themselves out of the pool, proud of their dripping bloody knees, a sign of time well-spent scrambling along the bottom.

Whether indoors or out, some of my adventure stories have been less successful than others. One of my very first pieces for NPR, was a report about whitewater canoeing. It wasn't timely; it had no great personalities; it wasn't particularly daring. As if this piece wasn't already destined for the radio dustbin, I chose to produce it without narration. I wanted to imitate a technique I'd heard a reporter that I admired use—there would be no scripting whatsoever, just the sounds of the river and the voices we recorded.

The result was a complete fiasco—six or so minutes of what a friend characterized as several toilets flushing. I give myself a couple of kudos for at least trying something different—and failing. But whoever edited this story dropped the ball. They should have told me, "You know what, Peter, this is just about the worst piece I've ever heard," and saved our listeners a couple of minutes of their lives.

It is often excruciating to play archival tape. When I was cleaning out my office some years ago, I came across the aforementioned Yosemite rock climbing stories I had done more than 20 years earlier. I made the mistake of cuing them up.

There was one section when a climber I had outfitted with a wireless mic (who had previously broken his spine in a cliff tumble) fell about 12 feet onto his back with a petrifying "umph." He was okay, but, tragically, another athlete I profiled for that report, free soloist John Bachar who used no ropes or other protection, would die in a fall years later.

My piece did have some compelling moments, but by and large it was wearisome. At the end of the story, the *All Things Considered* host said, "And tomorrow on our program in Part II of his series on rock climbers, Peter Breslow . . ." No please! Make it stop!

Times change. Radio styles change. There is no way in the world one of our news magazines would dedicate that much air time to a garden-variety rock climbing story in this day and age. Nor should they.

In reality, audio stories have now gotten shorter and longer at the same time. With the panoply of media available and our ever more limited attention spans, the NPR news magazines have demanded briefer pieces. However, the customized listening of podcasts has developed an audience for longer stories. We have entered a golden age of having and eating our audio cake.

# Chapter 31

# Cowboys on Everest

One early spring day a phone call is routed to me. It is a mountain climber pitching an Everest expedition traveling through China and Tibet that he will embark on in August with a team from Wyoming. They call themselves Cowboys On Everest and their trek, The Wyoming Centennial Everest Expedition, is to commemorate the 100th anniversary of Wyoming's statehood.

Whatever. Another Everest expedition. Who cares about Wyoming's statehood anniversary? But then the mountaineer on the line speaks a version of this magic sentence: "And we'll have a satellite phone with us so we could talk to you from base camp." Ding. Ding. Ding. Ding. Instantaneous scheming commences.

This is 1988, well before climbing Everest has become something any chump with a down jacket would try, and before remote communications via satellite phones has become so commonplace. "What if," I ask him, "I could convince NPR to send me along to cover you guys? Could I come?" The Cowboys quickly say yes, as does my *ATC* executive producer, Neal Conan, if, he adds, NPR can come up with the money to cover my expenses.

Months and months and months go by, and I hear nothing from my bosses about the funding. As summer arrives, I give up hope and move on to other projects. Then, with four days to go before the Cowboys depart for China, NPR says yes; they will pony up the finances for the two-to-three-month expedition. I can go.

I make a beeline for the nearest REI, plop down $1,500 and say,

"Gimme all your long underwear." Actually, there is an extensive list of necessities, many of which are new to me: Dachstein mittens, jumars, prescription glacier glasses, super gaiters, water bottle insulators and a down suit that looks like it came out of the closet of the Stay-Puft Marshmallow Man.

It's a mad dash, and there is barely time to register that I am the most novice of mountaineers, who has done no high-altitude training or any training, really, aside from my usual weekend bike rides.

Pretty quickly, I find myself sitting in a bus with 35 climbers at the end of an abandoned runway at the Beijing international airport. A disco version of an old Four Tops song is playing faintly over the bus's crackly speakers.

As I look out the window through a monsoon downpour, expedition mountaineering director Bob Skinner pulls a little clear shower cap over the peak of his already soggy cowboy hat. Other team members struggle to cover nearly 40-thousand pounds of gear with plastic sheeting. Water is dripping from the end of every nose. A cooler falls off the pile and breaks open, sending cans of beer and soda pop rolling across the tarmac. This is going to be a very long expedition.

I glance around the bus at the people who will be my companions for the next few months and grow a little nervous. They all—men and women—look so chiseled. Will I be able to keep up?

The expedition leader is Courtney Skinner, a hawk-nosed tobacco-chewing horse packer, who with his brother Bob, runs a wilderness school in Wyoming. The Chinese tell Courtney the gear at the end of the runway will be traveling 1,800 miles without us, via trucks overland across China, while we continue to Lhasa, Tibet, on a Chinese airline.

From there, it will be bus and truck to the Everest base camp. Timing is crucial. We are trying to thread a needle here, to climb the mountain between the end of the summer monsoon in late August and the onset of the winter jet stream, which drops down to Everest height (29,032 ft.) in mid-October.

Our sponsor on the ground is the Chinese Mountaineering Association (CMA). The CMA people, it turns out, don't know terribly much about mountaineering. As a matter of fact, only one of our five or so hosts has ever been to the Himalayas. That's the big guy we call Jaws.

From Beijing we fly to the city of Chengdu, then on to Lhasa where the Cowboys' sullen mood improves markedly in the thin crisp air of the 12,000-foot high city. As I get to know the climbers, I am very impressed.

Courtney Skinner has assembled an eclectic crew of teachers, doctors, even artists—people, he figures, who not only climb well, but can bring their experiences back to their Wyoming communities. There are several female mountaineers, one of whom the Cowboys hope will become the first American woman to summit Everest, a prize that brings not only boasting rights, but also perhaps some endorsement deals that will help defray expedition costs.

In Lhasa, we wait for our meandering trucks to arrive. It is an enchanted place, full of chanting, bald-headed monks spinning prayer wheels, and home to the enormous Potala Palace, the former winter residence of the exiled Dalai Lama. Its royal white and maroon storybook presence sits in stark contrast to the scowling, grim, cement Chinese architecture that pocks the city.

We kill time touring Lhasa and eating yak burgers. One afternoon, I hike up a small peak behind a burned out monastery, likely torched by the Chinese. Near the top I see an elderly woman with a young child. She beckons me to follow her to her little hut. Inside she shows me her simple shrine to the Dalai Lama. I give her a tiny photo of him I have and she places it on the altar. I ask to take her picture, but she shakes her head no; and as I leave, she gets back to work churning goat milk in an old wooden tub.

A couple of days pass and still no trucks, so we begin the approximately 380-mile overland trek to the Everest base camp, hoping to cross paths with our gear along the way. The vehicle the Chinese serve up for this first phase of our journey is vintage bus-plunge material. The seats are soaking wet and moldy; there is less legroom than ultrabasic-economy class; the tires are bald, and the gas tank is inside the bus with us.

Within the first half hour of the day's 14-hour ride. we are pulled over by two jeep-loads of Chinese police. It seems that our bags are piled too high on top of the bus, and we snapped a telephone line when departing Lhasa. Our driver has his license revoked and is then issued a temporary permit so that he can continue to drive us. Twenty minutes later, heading up our first mountain pass, the bus sputters and dies.

Vehicle repaired, we chug over 16,000-foot passes, past giant glaciers, then down onto green plateaus and along a huge lake, turned stunning aquamarine from glacial milk. In the distance, we spot the black tents of nomads, a plume of smoke rising from their yak-dung fires.

Whenever the bus stops, we are immediately engulfed by a crowd of kids who seem to pop out of the blue and have great fun playing with balloons we've brought along to entertain them. If we pass through a tiny village, there are sure to be multicolored prayer flags flapping, each flutter sending good will wafting.

Later that day, we come to the first of many landslides. Locals tell us this is the worst monsoon season in 100 years and the often impossible Tibetan roads have become virtually impassable.

Our driver is very good, nosing past other vehicles trapped axle-deep in the muck, negotiating boulder fields that would be ludicrous to ever call roads. With a perpetual cigarette dangling not far from that gas tank, he turns around and gives us a *that-ain't-nothin'* glance and plows ahead.

Sometimes, when the bus gets stuck, we have to jump out to push, and on the sharpest cliffside switchbacks, we all move to the high side of the vehicle to avoid the aforementioned bus plunge. The Cowboys pass around a bottle of Baileys Irish Cream, but I fake taking a swig. A few days later when a number of the group come down with intestinal and respiratory problems, I am glad of my caution, especially since it is very difficult to recover from illness at high altitude.

After a few days, we arrive in the village of Xegar, the last stop before base camp. Still no trucks. I am reading *Seven Years in Tibet*, Heinrich Harrer's account of traveling through the region in the 1940's without food or proper clothing. Periodically, he is attacked by wild dogs, pursued by authorities and confronted by bandits. I wonder if the CMA was escorting him also. At this point, for all we know, our gear could be buried in a landslide somewhere.

Exploring Xegar while we cool our heels, I notice some interesting syntax. A warning posted on a hotel wall reads, "Forbid drunken, quarrel, rude action, etc. Taken to the police station if anyone did." Back in the town of Shigatse one lunch place was named, *Restaurant of Turn Around Smilingly*. Has Yoda been through here teaching ESL?

Early one morning we are shaken out of bed by tremors from an earthquake that has mainly struck India and Nepal. The next day, as talk turns to human sacrifice, finally, finally, our equipment trucks rumble into town. The gear has spent nearly a month in boxes soaked by the monsoon. When we open up our stuff, we find squishy down jackets and ice axes alive with white slimy goo. Still, we are overjoyed to be underway. Almost.

Not far down the road there is a problem. The earthquake, we discover, has knocked out a good 15-foot section of the bridge over the Luoluo River that flows outside Xegar—the river between us and Mt. Everest. With frontier gusto, Bob Skinner says, "Let's fill in the hole."

To the Tibetans' great delight, we strapping mountain women and men form a chain and begin passing rocks down the line and chucking them into the frothing, rain-swollen water, trying to fill the gap between the bank and the remaining portion of the bridge so our trucks can make it over. After an hour or two, the hole is, if anything, a bit wider.

Plan B: Ford the river. We watch as a truck on the opposite shore tries to make it across. In the middle of the torrent it is swamped, the chocolate-colored water rising around it towards the cab windows. The people inside scramble to the roof just as the river starts flowing over the steering wheel. There are two men and a boy around 10 or 11-years-old. I fear I am about to witness a triple drowning.

It is pouring. Amid the tumult and screaming, bystanders mount a rescue attempt. Somehow a rope is strung across the river and the boy is tied on. As rescuers tug on the line, the boy bobs in and out of the raging brown soup, gasping for breath every time his head pops out of the water. After an eternity, the kid, who never even seems to cry, and the two men are pulled to safety. We table the fording the river idea.

The next day the river is down, and we convince our truck drivers to make an attempt. It's successful and we continue the final leg to the mountain. At 2:30 a.m., after a torturous undulating ride featuring multiple barf bag sessions, we pull into base camp at 17,000 feet and pass out. It has been almost a month since we left the U.S.

# Chapter 32

# Top of the World

In the morning I wake up, look out my tent and, there it is, Chomolungma, as the Tibetans call it, Goddess Mother of the World. The mountain is so huge, so white and perfect against a clear, azure Tibetan sky that it looks fake, like some gigantic slide that's being projected. After weeks crossing China and Tibet, I'm really here—close to the top of the world.

One good thing about all the delays in arriving is that team members have had a chance to gradually get used to the thin air. Some people acclimatize better than others, and I seem to do pretty well; but one Cowboy is never able to adapt and has to be sent home.

My tentmate is Mr. Kong, the only Chinese member of our expedition. The Skinners decided to pair up the two oddballs. He is a very friendly geologist who wears polyester pants and street shoes while the rest of us run around in space age fabrics built for lightness and warmth. Mr. Kong does not speak English very well, so every evening we have little lessons in the tent. I tell him I'm going to start charging, and he says then he wants his money's worth, so I better include all the dirty words.

The sat phone that has made my presence possible is housed in a big white hut. It can be used in the mornings and evenings, when we fire up the generator. You can send and receive calls. The phone rings—a delicate, little, Princess model—and someone says, "It's for you." At 17,000 feet, "It's for you."

In our current era of modern, lightweight, mobile communications, this doesn't sound that exceptional, but back in 1988 it was pretty exciting. I can use the sat phone to file stories (only phone quality) back to Washington and occasionally speak to my girlfriend. But you can't schmooze for long: it costs the equivalent of $40 per minute in today's dollars.

We are camped on the only patch of grass around. This is the moraine of the main Rongbuk glacier. A few miles from here, the icy portion of the glacier begins, leading to Everest's North Face. Our route will take us up a 2,000-foot snow-and-ice wall called the North Col, then on to the northeast ridge and ultimately the summit. It is a long slow slog, the same itinerary on which British climbers, George "Because it's there" Mallory and Andrew Irvine, disappeared in 1924. Courtney Skinner hopes to follow Mallory's plan, skipping the last part.

About 15 miles up the mountain, we establish advanced base camp (ABC) at 21,000 feet. We have no Sherpas or porters, the climbers must carry their personal gear on their backs. Yaks transport the heaviest loads, like propane tanks and tents, but only as far as ABC.

The yak herders are tiny, gentle-looking guys with braided black hair, wearing bracelets, turquoise earrings and blue sneakers. Their names translate to things like Thunderbolt and Wish-Granting Gem. They pop into the cook tent after dinner and listen along with us to The Talking Heads on our boombox. Then they sing their own songs and I record them. Later they ask to hear the cassette again and again.

This being well before the world became so small with digital connectivity, our Tibetan friends look on in wonder as we transmit photos of them to a television network in New York, probably not understanding that millions of people on the other side of the planet will soon catch a glimpse of their lives.

If base camp first appeared to be the end of the earth to me, advanced base camp is the dark side of Pluto. The big jagged shoulder of Everest is just to our left, across the glacier. Straight ahead is the white icy wall of the North Col. Closer, the mountain is both more wonderful and terrifying, its craggy features now much better defined. At night we hear avalanches thundering down its flanks. Days and weeks pass as the team establishes the route on the Col and drags up supplies.

At ABC the air is much colder and thinner. Sometimes simply lying in your tent you suddenly find yourself gasping for breath. At night the temperature falls to 10 below; and when you wake up in the morning, you discover your nighttime breaths are still with you, transformed into frost that covers your sleeping bag and tent walls.

Sleeping is very difficult. You get headaches. The cold air and altitude dehydrate you, so you have to force down more and more liquids. You don't want to get out of your two sleeping bags in the middle of the night, so you keep a pee bottle handy. (Just don't mix it up with your water bottle in the dark.) As you sleep, your tongue becomes dried and cracked and ends up sticking to the roof of your mouth. Your lips, perpetually blistered by the environment, seal together during the night and become a bloody mess as they split apart in the morning.

It is not possible to bathe above base camp, which means you go a good two weeks between wash-ups. When you finally change your long underwear, your decayed epidermis peels off like snakeskin.

All the while, I am producing stories—profiling members of the expedition, detailing the lives of the yak herders, talking about high-altitude life on the mountain and strategies for the summit bid. When it is time to file, I have to hike back down to base camp and the sat phone.

Aside from the altitude, the route is not difficult, but I am warned to stay alert. Not too long ago a couple of Japanese climbers were killed by a toppling ice serac. At the base it seems like the Caribbean, all that oxygen and 35-degree temperatures. I can even heat up some water and bathe.

Being a journalist on this expedition presents some complications. As a member of a team that is at times performing some risky maneuvers, I cannot simply be a silent observer. Everyone depends on each other and that includes me. While I do not have the mountaineering skills to be a lead climber, I am expected to carry my weight with more mundane tasks, like hauling water from the one spot in the stream that is not frozen over, a half mile above ABC.

There are, however, times when I have to separate myself from my teammates. Disagreements have percolated about the expedition's leadership and decision-making. As uncomfortable as it may be, I have to report on this. I remember receiving a letter from a listener after I returned to the States admonishing me for criticizing the Skinner brothers, as though I were a fleece-wrapped Benedict Arnold. I felt bad about it but also knew this was something that was part of my job.

Two months into the expedition the descending jet stream clock is ticking down, and tensions continue to rise. Once those winds hit, a summit attempt will be very difficult. The trip is lasting so long—thanks to the Chinese bureaucracy and natural disasters—that I meet recently arrived climbers from other expeditions, who have heard some of my Everest reports on NPR before leaving the States.

After filing stories to Washington from base camp, and a couple of days there of R&R, I make my way back up to ABC for a stay I hope will include a summit attempt by the team. The food up here is not bad—lots of stews and soups, hash browns and candy bars. But no one has much of an appetite at 21,000 feet, so you have to force yourself to eat. Still, we are all losing weight, burning thousands of calories just to get through the day. I will drop close to 20 pounds before we head home. At some point I have this entrepreneurial inspiration: *The Everest Eating & Dieting Spa: Chow down as much as you possibly can and still lose weight!*

Once the route up the North Col is fixed, I decide to attempt it. With an ice ax, a mini-cassette recorder and a lapel mic, I narrate as I climb, hoping to turn this ascent into a piece. I also have an avalanche beeper in my pocket. My climbing partner tells me, "With this thing, if you're buried under six feet of snow we look for ya. Under 12 feet, we just call the family."

Clipping into the fixed line that has been anchored all the way up the route, I start out. Soon my lungs are pleading but I trudge on. It is tough, very tough, but not impossible. I find a rhythm—step, three breaths, step, three breaths, kick in with my crampons, plant the ax into the ice, step, three breaths—all the while recording.

If I have any meager claim to fame at NPR (at least among the old-timers) it is this excruciatingly heavy breathing that I put on the radio—along with a gasping rendition of Sonny Boy Williamson's *Help Me* that I sang for inspiration along the way.

Hours pass. I am in the zone, dragging myself past enormous seracs and pure white overhanging cornices, then up what feels like an almost 90-degree wall of ice. It is a challenge to try to narrate as I go, to edit this climb in my head so that when I listen back to the tape later on, I will hear more than just panting, cursing and off-key singing. As is often the case when I have done something less than cautious while reporting, the fact that I'm working takes my mind off whatever risks might be involved.

Just shy of the Col's summit, I reach the crux of the climb, a 12-or-so-foot wide crevasse that looks to be maybe a hundred feet deep. The only way across is a bridge that the team has constructed. This is, however, no Golden Gate. It is more of a ladder, fashioned out of two climbing ropes, with aluminum snow pickets, usually used for anchoring things down on the glacier, serving as the rungs.

You go over on your hands and knees, which means you are staring into the frigid maw the entire time. Wearing heavy gear, a camera dangling from my neck, lugging a rope and climbing hardware, with sharp toothy crampons on the souls of my boots, and quivering with exhaustion, I am less than my usual agile self. With each hesitant step forward, the bridge tips awkwardly. About midway across, I slip and collapse onto my chest, which turns off the tape recorder in the pocket of my jumpsuit.

I press record once I am over the bridge and scamper the rest of the way to the top of the Col, 23,000 feet. Although I have started to harbor fantasies of being able to summit with the rest of the team (they are protective of their most inexperienced member), I have achieved the goal I had set for myself at the start of the expedition.

To the south below me, the jagged peaks of Nepal glint like shark's teeth in the late afternoon sun. Straight ahead, closer than ever, the steel gray stone pyramid that is Everest's summit, blown almost clear of snow from the high winds above. I feel powerful and powerless at the same time and understand a bit better why locals call Everest the Goddess Mother of the World.

My teammates leave me little time for contemplation. It will soon be dark and it is a long way back down. Twelve hours after leaving advanced base camp I stumble back in, borderline incoherent. The Cowboys greet me in the cook tent with pats on the back and congratulations. After more than two months I feel I've proven myself with this group. I grab a couple of spoonfuls of mashed potatoes, head to my tent and face plant.

The audio I transmit back to D.C. is only phone quality, which makes it very difficult to understand, but as one colleague tells me after I return, "I had no idea what you were saying, but I couldn't stop listening." That makes me feel terrific, that I have done my job of bringing listeners to a place they would probably never get to visit on their own. I feel privileged. I am actually being paid to do something for which most of my Cowboy teammates have scrimped and saved.

As we near a month at ABC and the team starts establishing upper camps, things turn glum in the dining tent. Each evening, 15 to 20 of us squeeze onto cold stone benches. The floor of the tent is rocky glacial moraine with probably 40 to 100 feet of ancient ice underneath. People look sun scorched, haggard and dazed, in red, yellow and blue jumpsuits and down parkas, chaotic hair sticking up in every direction. Conversation has dwindled down to the essentials, "Has the water boiled yet?"

Even though no one is hungry, dinner is still the highlight of the day—a reason to get out of our tents for a couple of hours. Basically, if you're not climbing, you're resting and conserving strength. We fill our thermal cups with beans and franks and mash them together with some macaroni and cheese. Someone comments that there are no civilizations that live above 17,000 feet. No shit. By 7:30 pm, the stone benches have grown too uncomfortable, so you head back to your tent and your fifth novel of the trip. *Lonesome Dove*, nice and thick, is a favorite.

In the days that follow, the team establishes a camp as high as 25,000 feet, and we are all getting summit fever. Then disaster hits. One-hundred-mile-an-hour winds smash the high camps, shredding tents and chasing climbers back down to ABC.

A few days later with a slight break in the weather, the team attempts another quick assent, but the winds return. It is too dangerous to continue, and everyone is too depleted to wait for another window. The Cowboys reach the only decision possible, to head home without the summit.

Back at base camp, disappointment quickly gives way to celebration as we break open the beer stash and begin a series of strange little parties each night after dinner in the cook tent. With the Sex Pistols blasting from the boombox, someone pulls out a barber's clippers and begins making creative work of the Cowboys scraggly beards and hair—racing stripes, white walls and Mohawks all around.

My now good friend Mr. Kong, his English somewhat improved, joins in the merrymaking, as do the yak herders. We are a collective, weathered, exhausted mess, but everyone is laughing. And as Johnny Rotten rants *Anarchy in the U.K.*, Cowboys, yak herders and Mr. Kong begin slam dancing. Our timing may have been off for reaching Everest's summit, but now we seem to have it down just fine.

·

Months after my return, I win a Peabody Award for my Everest stories, and my boss Neal Conan tells me, "That will go in the obit," which is a little uncomfortable to think about. In fact, that obituary almost arrives prematurely.

One evening the following summer D.C. is hit with a massive thunderstorm. After it moves through, my buddy Jim says, "Let's go tubing in Rock Creek." The next thing I know I am standing on the bank looking on as the usual trickle of the nearby stream in D.C.'s Rock Creek Park has been transformed into a foamy raging surge of storm run-off. It is 8 pm and almost dark, but I hop onto my giant inflated inner tube and take the plunge.

Immediately, I'm in trouble. A big brown wave smacks me in the face, washing off my glasses and turning everything hazy in the dying light. Jim is a much more talented tuber and has already vanished downstream. I float toward a dark mass I assume is a boulder off which I'll be able to bounce.

As I get closer, I realize this is not a rock but a strainer, a mass of tangled branches stuck in the creek. I hit it and lose my tube. The force of the water pins me against the limbs, and I am just barely able to keep my head above the torrent as I swallow gulps of the sickeningly sweet polluted Rock Creek water. I cling to a branch for all I'm worth, but there is no way I can withstand the force of the stream.

My only chance of saving myself is to let the current carry me under the strainer and hope that the branches aren't embedded in the muck below, which would allow me to pass beneath without getting trapped underwater. Taking a deep breath, I release the branch and let my body go limp.

Once again, luck is with me. I float under the twisted tree limbs, pop out the other side and drag myself onto the bank retching. A few minutes later, Jim, fearing the worst, comes humping up the road with his inner tube slung over his shoulder. He breathes a sigh of relief and asks simply, "How's it going?"

For years afterwards, I can still taste that cloying stream and find myself sometimes wondering if maybe I really died that night and I am now in an afterlife that is remarkably similar to the one I left. The ignominy of drowning in usually dinky Rock Creek after surviving Everest is not lost on me either.

Interviewing Cowboy
on Everest climber Fred
Riedman, Everest base
camp, Tibet, 1988

# Chapter 33

# Got My Mojo Workin'

The blues has been a life obsession that I have forced onto NPR's air-waves at every opportunity. Scott Simon can't stand the music; he's a show tunes kind of guy, and yet I have twisted his arm to feature the blues on *Weekend Edition* so often that people regularly come up to him and thank him for keeping the genre alive. To this Scott replies, "I despise the blues. It's my producer who makes me do all those interviews."

Scott has gotten his revenge, though. Not only did he once introduce me in person to Stephen Sondheim, he somehow unearthed a copy of the late composer's high-school-yearbook photo and stuck it on the bulletin board in my office with the inscription, "You're the kind of guy who used to give me wedgies. Eat shit, Stephen."

The blues first appeared to me my freshman year in college via Louie J. Suckle, my across the hall dormmate. Louie was a late-night DJ on the campus station who introduced me to fabled bluesman Robert Johnson as well as a Hohner Blues Harp in a handy soft blue plastic case. Although, I do remember as a kid once getting a red plastic harmonica I really didn't care for ("I don't want a harmonica for Chanukah"), this time something just clicked. I bought the records of Little Walter, Sonny Boy Williamson, James Cotton and Paul Butterfield and drove my roommates crazy as I tried to imitate what I heard.

At some point, I developed enough technique to play in low rent bar bands with names like Jay Walker and the Pedestrians (I was one of the

Pedestrians), The Arthur Cable Blues Band, the Pioneer Valley Hokum Boys, Truck Patch and today, The Slidewinders.

The pocket-sized instrument was just perfect when I dropped out of college and hitchhiked around the U.S. You can play it while you're driving. And if your legs are long enough and you can steer with your knees, you can use both hands!

With my harp, I've been able to cozy up to people in far-flung places—from serenading those kids Scott and I befriended in war-time Kosovo, to jamming with the yak herders at the Everest base camp (and let me tell you—blowing at 17,000 feet is a workout), to wailing away in the stone inner courtyard (with great acoustics) of a caravan-serai hotel while on assignment with *ATC* host Robert Siegel in Diyar-bakir in southeastern Turkey. I can't imagine what the Kurds who live in that part of the world thought of my rendition of *Cross Road Blues* or whatever it was I played that evening.

I've had the good fortune to have visited and on occasion done stories about some of this country's few remaining old-time blues bars before they disappeared—taverns like Tabby's Blues Box in Baton Rouge, Gip's Place outside of Birmingham, and Lee's Unleaded Blues on Chi-cago's South Side—all of them downhome spots where the bartenders made you feel welcome and the music was as genuine and houserockin' as it gets.

In the early 1990's, I went down to Chulahoma, Mississippi, for a pro-file on hill country blues guitarist Junior Kimbrough. He had a back-woods juke joint outside of town. It was an intimate place heated by a wood stove in the middle of the single room. (Sadly, the spot has since burned down.) When we showed up on a Sunday afternoon, a stately older woman, still dressed in what appeared to be her church outfit, occupied a chair front and center so that she could immerse herself in Junior's raw, deep, haunting blues.

The scene gave me goosebumps and the music was hypnotic, but we ran into issues when we started to interview Junior. Between his deep Southern accent and problematic dental work, we found him very difficult to understand. It was tough finding usable tape for our final piece.

A year or so after my trip to his roadhouse Junior made an appearance at a blues club in the D.C. area. I found him at the bar and reminded him of my visit and bought him a beer. We sat down at a table to talk, but I'm sorry to report that once again I had no idea what Junior was saying, so we both just smiled a lot and sipped our drinks. The music he played that night was spellbinding and put the audience into a trance.

Of the array of musical masters I've gotten to interview, Chuck Berry was a one-of-a-kind. I was backstage at a theater in Washington prior to a performance waiting for the man to appear. I had been warned that you can never really be certain that Chuck will show up for an interview until he is standing right in front of you.

We waited and waited, even ordering a pizza to be delivered when dinner time had come and gone. Still no Chuck.

As I was eyeing a second slice, in he strode, strapping, in a bright red shirt with a blonde date on his arm. I just remember my hand disappearing into his huge mitt as we shook hands.

Then Chuck Berry sat down, stretched his long legs up onto a table and said something like, "What do you guys want to talk about?"

*Roll Over Beethoven, Nadine, Johnny B Goode, Rock and Roll Music, Sweet Little Sixteen, Maybellene.* Here I was, hanging out with the man who primed the pump for all the rock and roll that followed.

Sometimes my job is just perfect.

There were other blues icons I spent some time with over the years who were delighted to share their history with a dedicated fan—Koko Taylor, J.B Hutto, Carey Bell Harrington and Junior Wells. Then there was Robert Junior Lockwood.

In my younger days, Robert Junior was scheduled to play at the campus bar at my college. I showed up hours early, and the musician was there nursing a drink.

We got to chatting, and he invited me to his room for some music

in the campus hotel, which was just upstairs from the bar. I had a harmonica with me and was excited at the thought that I might get to play
with the man who had a direct lineage back to Robert Johnson, who
had taught him guitar.

Upstairs he opened his guitar case and pulled out what I remember as an electric 12-string. I reached into my pocket for my harp and
asked if we could jam. My hoped-for blues brother shut that down
pretty quickly.

"I don't want to play with no harmonica. I've played with too many
fuckin' harmonicas. Put that thing away."

That experience didn't diminish my enthusiasm for the blues and its
transformative power. A moment that still lingers is being in a Chicago
blues club in 1992. Sitting slumped at a table looking frail and tiny was
a bald-headed older gentleman. It was barrelhouse piano great Sun-
nyland Slim, well into his 80's at the time.

Shuffling with difficulty, he was escorted to an upright piano on a
small stage. Then a switch was thrown, decades disappeared, and Sun-
nyland Sim was a young man again, pounding away at the keyboard.
After three or four rollicking songs, the light was turned off, and Slim
was once more an old man being led back to his seat. He died about
three years later.

As I've mentioned, much of my blues-bonding at NPR has been with
correspondent John Burnett, certainly public radio's greatest harmonica player—I mean the man is of professional caliber. And at 6' 7",
undoubtedly, its tallest. On our reporting trips, each of us makes sure
to pack a harp in the key of C or A so we can jam.

My most surreal blues experience occurred with John deep in the
jungle of the Petén territory of northern Guatemala. We were there
among the howler monkeys, jaguars, and scarlet macaws to profile an
effort by archaeologist David Freidel to preserve and defend the site
of the ancient Mayan city of El Perú-Waká from tomb raiders—looters who steal and sell historic artifacts to unscrupulous or unsuspect-
ing dealers and collectors.

It's a rough part of the world you can barely reach with a four-wheel drive, where drug smugglers often roam with impunity.

A garrison of Guatemalan soldiers tasked with apprehending the cocaine traffickers and helping guard the sites was stationed near Freidel's camp in the jungle. The archeologist's outpost included a screened in porch where we had our meals.

It turned out Freidel was just as much of a blues nut as John and me and a pretty good guitar player. One evening after dinner we all pulled out our instruments and started jamming. Then the strangest scene unfolded. As we glanced around after finishing a song, we could see in the eerie glow of lantern light the faces of a dozen young Guatemalan soldiers emerging from the surrounding darkness.

They pressed up against the porch screens listening to us howl *Hoochie Coochie Man*, or maybe it was *Got My Mojo Workin'*. We could only begin to imagine what was going through their minds. Perhaps these descendants of the Maya would tell their children about that odd night, and someday we would become mythical like Quetzalcóatl, the feathered serpent deity thought to inhabit the region.

# Chapter 34

# Animal Planet

Everyone likes animal stories. Just look at your Facebook or TikTok feeds. On *Weekend Edition* when we do an interview about a lactose intolerant koala or a labradoodle that speaks Gaelic, we know listeners will make sure their earbuds are fitting snugly. Take for example:

## SNAKES ON THE FLOOR

On the southern gulf coast of Florida, there once lived a man named Bill Haast, who made a career of extracting venom from the most dangerous snakes in the world for use in medical research and for anti-venom.

When I visited him in 1999, he was 88 years old and as spry as a kid. Within 10 minutes of my arrival, he dragged me over a five-foot-high stone wall into an outdoor snake pit where he was raising eastern diamondback rattlers, the largest venomous snake in North America. He was intent on showing me just how close one could bring a microphone to the serpents. He called them gentlemen snakes.

I got about two feet from one of them, coiled and rattling between two palm trees. Its frantic sound would have been musical if I hadn't been so petrified. But that wasn't nearly close enough for Haast. He goaded this scaredy-cat reporter to get closer and closer to the vibrating diamondback. Finally, when my mic was just two inches away, the animal had had enough and quicker than the blink of an eye—thwack—it struck the padded end of my microphone leaving venomous dribbles.

Welcome to the Miami Serpentarium Laboratory. The Miami part was left over from the original Serpentarium where, beginning in the late 1940's, Haast honed his serpent-handling skills. Around this time too, he started injecting himself weekly with diluted cobra venom to build up his immunity to bites. On this day as I watched, Haast's wife, Nancy, shot him up with a cocktail that helped protect him from some 32 varieties of poison.

Haast was dressed all in white: white shoes, white pants, white belt, white shirt, all matching a full head of white hair framing an astonishingly unlined face. The man's blood was so potent it had been used as an anti-venom more than 20 times. A plaque in his office presented by President Gerald Ford commemorated the occasion in 1976 when Haast's blood saved two people in the same hospital on the same day.

When I interviewed him, he figured he had been bitten some 168 times, and his hands sure showed it. Several of his fingers were little more than stubs where the poison had destroyed his flesh.

Except for the diamondbacks outside, Haast's 200 or so snakes resided in pizza-box-shaped aluminum containers in his lab. Once every two weeks each snake got to see the light of day just long enough to be fed and have its venom extracted by biting into a rubber membrane attached to a beaker.

In those containers were kraits, copperheads, coral snakes, green tree snakes, boomslangs, Egyptian cobras, spitting cobras, monocled cobras and a snake-phobe's worst nightmare—an eight-foot-long black mamba. This guy was so dangerous that it had a lock on its pizza box. These reptiles provided a good living for Haast and his wife. Back then a gram of boomslang venom sold for $6000, Haast told me, although it could take hundreds of extractions to produce a single gram.

I wasn't going to get out of there without witnessing an extraction, so Haast pulled a brownish four-foot-long monocled cobra from its cozy container. Writhing and hissing, the snake was not happy.

Haast feinted with his left hand to distract the snake and moved his right into position to grab the animal behind its hood, now flared, revealing the single eye-like markings that give the monocled cobra its name. With his flowing white hair and quick arm movements, Haast looked like a conductor leading an orchestra composed of one very ornery squiggly musician.

At some point, the snake slithered onto the floor and tried to gain some traction on the smooth linoleum. Panicked, I danced around, trying to record the scene with my mic while keeping clear of the fangs.

With a fixed gaze, Haast reached down and grabbed the cobra by the tail as it flailed wildly, seeking something to strike. It seemed impossible for him not to be bitten, but Haast was just slightly quicker than the serpent, anticipating the snake's movements. At long last, he was able to grab its neck and guide its fangs into the rubbery membrane through which the venom flowed and flowed. I always had the sneaking suspicion that Haast had let that snake fall to the floor on purpose so he could give me a bit of a show. It worked. I was impressed.

An octogenarian bundle of energy, the snake handler wouldn't make claims that his weekly venom injections and occasional bites represented a prickly path to the fountain of youth, but he told me if he made it to 100, well, then maybe it was true. Bill Haast died in 2011, six months after celebrating his 100th birthday.


### ELEPHANTS AND RHINOS AND TIGERS, OH MY

I once got to go on a Rhino Roundup in the Terai lowlands of Chitwan National Park in south-central Nepal. We were several teams atop 15 Asian elephants—the one animal a rhinoceros won't charge—trying to track down a single rhino. The roundup was part of a program to capture and transport some greater one-horned rhinos from Chitwan, where there was an abundance, about 200 miles northeast to Bardia National Park, where poachers had decimated the population.

Under the direction of our elephant drivers, known as mahouts, we fanned out in search of a rhino to apprehend. Once we spotted our quarry, he was encircled and a marksman shot it with a tranquilizer gun.

The animal ran off before the drugs kicked in, so there ensued a mad scramble to track it down because if it collapsed and lay in the forest too long, it could suffocate under its own weight. The mahouts quickly discovered him; he was down but okay.

After lots of shouting and sweating, the beast was boxed up into an enormous wooden crate for transport to Bardia National Park. When he awoke, he was not a happy herbivore. Sound recordist Bill McQuay was able to capture the moment in stereo as the hungover animal thrashed and pounded the side of his crate. It was hair-raising audio.

On that same journey to the Terai region, we documented efforts to help preserve Bengal tiger habitats and reduce fatal encounters between the animals and villagers hunting for firewood in the forest. While we were there reporting the story, a tiger killed and ate a local woman as she was out collecting wood. It was a bit unnerving to be in the jungle and get out of our jeep or off our elephant and be told that tigers were likely watching us. Our guides warned us to stay close.

As we neared the end of our trip, I still had not seen a single big cat, and I was desperate to spot that rippling luminescent black and orange creature moving through the forest. Ultimately, I enlisted the aid of Danny Tamang, whom everyone told me was the best guide at Chitwan Park. Also accompanying us on the elephant was a former big game hunter turned naturalist. With such expertise, I felt certain my luck would change. But as I was warned, you never see a tiger unless it wants to be seen.

We spent a full day crashing through the kapok forest, wading through streams and slogging over tall grasses. At one point, we heard an agitated elephant trumpeting in the distance. We raced over and did find a tiger; alas, it was a dead six-month-old cub curled up in the grass, likely killed by a territorial adult male or from a poacher's poison.

With the sun setting, we disappointedly headed back to our hotel, where I was greeted by tourists from San Diego whom I had seen at the start of the day. That morning they and their run-of-the-mill mahout had headed out of our lodge to the east on their search for a tiger, while my experts—with 70 years of experience between them—and I had headed west. The tourists had been lucky. "Did you see a tiger?" one of them asked. I told her no. "You should have come with us," she beamed. "We got really close to one."

# Chapter 35

# The Ends of the Earth

The National Science Foundation (NSF) is the gatekeeper for journalists wanting to head to the South Pole and in 2008 they opened up a couple of slots for me and reporter Daniel Zwerdling.

In a case study of cosmic simultaneity, at the same moment that I was at the United States Antarctic base at McMurdo Station, my wife Jessica was a producer on a completely unrelated NPR assignment on the Antarctic Peninsula, 2,500 miles northwest. I have always kidded her that since she just barely made it to the continent—it was only the peninsula, for Pete's sake—it didn't really count. Still, she is winning the continent contest 7 to 6.

Daniel and I traveled from Christchurch, New Zealand, by military transport to McMurdo. As we deplaned, we had to lug all our own gear. I schlepped fat bags on each shoulder, bulging with layers upon layers of expedition-caliber clothing as well as all my audio paraphernalia. Dangling around my neck was a high-end camera entrusted to me by NPR, with the mandate to shoot lots and lots of photos.

Our aircraft had a set of steep no-nonsense steps to negotiate. Wearing heavy boots and a giant red parka that could conceal the offensive line of the Green Bay Packers, I must have bent my neck just a bit too far, and the camera slid over my head, sailing lens first straight into the ice below.

Holy shit! I have not even set foot on the continent and I've already managed to destroy my camera. Panicked, I descended the steps, reached down and picked it up expecting to find a spider web of cracks in the lens. Miraculously, the metal lens hood that extended past the optics had protected it. I'd dodged an icy bullet.

Years before I'd had another case of butterfingers with an NPR camera. I was in Tennessee doing a story about The Body Farm, where donated corpses are left to rot so that scientists can measure the speed of their decomposition. The statistics they gather are used to help police with their forensics work, such as determining how long a murdered husband has been lying in his basement with his wife's rolling pin next to his cracked skull.

For my story, I stood in a field over a body that was almost liquefied, dutifully recording the sound of the flies hovering around the corpse. I was also snapping pictures when, for a moment, I lost my concentration and the camera slipped from my hand, right into the fetid, maggot-infested body with a sickening squish. In the end NPR would not run the photographs; they said they were too gruesome. My photos from the Antarctica trip did make it onto our website.

From the McMurdo base we flew to the Pole, a glistening, white, pancake-flat, ice-encrusted landscape where the sun perched high in the sky around the clock at that time of year. Look out your window at 2 a.m. and it could be 2 p.m.

The US South Pole Station was brand spanking new at the time. It featured a pool table, a basketball court and private rooms with telephones. I remember excitedly dialing my 8-year-old daughters, "Hi girls, I'm calling you from the South Pole!" "That's nice, Daddy. We've got to get ready for school, okay? Love you."

Outdoors, despite the perpetual sunshine, the weather was 50 below with the wind chill factor. Venturing out involved an exhausting process of putting on seven layers of gear. One day as Danny and I were interviewing a Polie on the ice, I had to take off my heavy outer glove to adjust the levels on my machine.

Despite wearing a liner glove, my hand quickly became painfully numb. Once again in my recording career I could hardly hold the microphone. As the interview went on and on, Danny finally noticed the pained look on my face and we headed indoors.

I felt like such a crybaby compared to the hearty crew that winters

183

over at the Pole when temperatures can reach 150 below zero with the wind chill. Once the last plane leaves in mid-February, there is no getting out until October (jet fuel would freeze), and for much of that time the sky remains pitch black.

Those who winter-over are carefully screened for sound health and mental stability. After that final flight departs, the remaining Polies settle in for their annual ritual—a screening of the 1951 sci-fi classic, *The Thing from Another Word*. It's the story of an alien from outer space that crash lands in the Arctic and terrorizes the earthlings. The film is set at the North Pole, not the South, but no matter, everyone is happily creeped out nonetheless. Winter veterans told us about the stress, wonder, and spirituality of those months in the frigid darkness, kind of like they were in outer space, they said.

Another surprise of Antarctica is that you can visit the hut near the McMurdo base occupied by British naval captain Robert Falcon Scott and his team during their ill-fated quest to become the first people to reach the South Pole. Scott and four others did make it to the Pole on January 17, 1912, only to find that Norwegian explorer Roald Amundsen had beaten them there by about a month. Depleted and dispirited, Scott's party died on the return trip; their bodies remain frozen somewhere out on the empty ice.

Dry, freezing temperatures have helped preserve what remained behind in Scott's hut, even 100 years later. There are cotton trousers and reindeer-fur boots the explorers wore, as well as tins of food and, hanging on a hook, a slab of seal meat that still very slowly drips fat.

The Antarctic historian on our expedition was a marine biologist from the University of Southern California named Daniel Manahan. He was a jolly and unassuming adventurer who risked his neck scuba diving under the ice in 29-degree water. He described the sensation as diving under clouds, which sounds poetic; but one mistake—like if you were to lose track of your access hole in the six-foot-thick ice— and you were a goner.

One day he took us zooming out on snowmobiles at 50 miles an hour

Interviewing a local, Antarctica, 2008

on the blinding-white frozen ocean, where we got to check out his global warming research and have an encounter with a 1000-pound Weddell seal.

Wielding axes and shovels, Manahan's graduate students had dug a hole in the ice and were collecting water samples to determine how our warming planet was affecting the tiniest of the local sea life. All of a sudden, an enormous, shiny, black nose with flared nostrils poked through the slushy water.

Everyone froze in place, and I scurried over with my mic, trying not to fall into the hole. It was a sound recordist's dream taping the seal as it oxygenated with huge splattering breaths, one after another after another. Once the animal had had its fill, it submerged for another 15-minute dive.

That trip to Antarctica leaves me just one more box to check on my continental collection—Australia, a place with probably more fantastical fauna than anywhere I've ever been.

**Chapter 36**

# Adios

Surprise, it took me so long to write this thing that I've retired! Now you can go back and reread this book putting everything in the past tense. After 39 years on the news locomotive, much of that time working weekends, I've decided to holster my digital razor blade.

Yes, a normal person would have waited until completing a nice round 40 years, which would have guaranteed a rent-subsidized condo at Nipper Golden Acres in Boca Raton. But I am done.

I am excited now only to follow the news stories that interest me and to open up the Sunday *New York Times* (the only hard copy newspaper I still get) and read it at my leisure without hunting for story ideas. Oh, and to sleep in on Saturdays and Sundays. As a fellow recent-retiree noted, "It's great not to have to crank out shit."

My last year at NPR coincided with the network turning 50 years old. It would be nice and symmetrical to say we entered middle age together, but I'd be lying. I beat NPR by a number of years.

My final year was also marked by the first and worst of the Covid pandemic, the height of the social justice movement, and the end of the tumultuous Trump presidency.

## TRUMP TURMOIL

The Trump years turned the news cycle up to warp speed. There had been nothing like it during my career. A weekly firehose of havoc. His erratic actions and incendiary tweets (until Twitter banned him) became so disruptive and unpredictable that we were forced to do more and more segments live in our weekend broadcasts so that pre-recorded interviews wouldn't become outdated by a 5 a.m. social media blast.

The first thing I would do upon waking up early on a Saturday or Sunday morning in preparation for line producing *Weekend Edition* would be to open up Twitter to see if the president had posted something that blew out a show segment. Often he had. Then we would scramble to grab someone to talk about it.

Trump was created by the media; he offered up outlandish behavior that many news outlets (NPR included) found just too tempting to ignore. He increased listener-viewer-readership and kept himself front and center. Far too often we let him set the agenda for our programs creating a vicious cycle that only fed off itself. It exhausted us.

Even though he was commanding the headlines and the airways (any publicity is good publicity, right?), Trump regarded most of us as "the enemy of the people" when we spoke the truth to his lies. (It took a while before NPR allowed us to call his untruths "lies" on the air).

In the end, Trump's words unleashed the hounds, giving license to those who already harbored animosity towards the media to act. Colleagues at Trump rallies were kept in pens, taunted and cursed at. NPR's security experts treated these events as if they were war zones. During the January 6th, 2021 insurrection at the US Capitol, journalists were assaulted and their equipment smashed.

The most horrifying was the 2018 *Capital Gazette* newspaper shooting in Annapolis, Maryland, in which five people were gunned down in their newsroom. Yes, the murderer had a long-held grievance against the *Gazette*, but it is hard to believe that Donald Trump's rants against news organizations didn't at least play a part in motivating that attack.

At this moment Trump is indicted, but hardly diminished, so who knows what's in store. As more than one pundit has pointed out, the Trump presidency put American democracy to the test. That exam is ongoing, but if in the end we pass, I'd like to think that the news media was at least partially responsible.

### RADIO IN THE TIME OF CORONA

When Covid-19 flattened the world in March of 2020 the big brains at NPR, especially the logistics and technical people, hardly missed a beat. They very quickly figured out ways for us to produce our programs while working from home—just going into the office on broadcast days and occasionally not even then. I was astounded at how seamless it all went.

With Zoom and a recording app, we were able to have our staff meetings and also conduct and record interviews remotely. It was much more technically challenging and time consuming than just waltzing into a studio and opening a mic, but we all got used to it pretty quickly. Listeners could hardly tell the difference, except when a host's dog went crazy over a squirrel out in the yard or when, say, a senior producer's wife turned on her Vitamix as Scott Simon was talking to some author, and said producer didn't have his Zoom connection muted.

Usually, high profile guests wanted us only to use Zoom audio for their interviews, no video, so that they wouldn't have to call in their make-up artist. But sometimes they didn't care, and it was fun for me to watch musicians like Elvis Costello or Richard Thompson chatting from their home music studios.

When we talked to singer Patty Smyth, who is married to John McEnroe, the tennis great poked his head in front of the camera to say hi while walking through the living room. Covid protocols created a certain informality that didn't normally happen with studio interviews, a feeling that we were all in this together. I mean, how often do you get to explain to musician Bonnie Raitt or actress Laura Linney how to upload their audio to you?

Despite the technical workarounds, there was a lot lost by not working in physical proximity to each other. I missed all those times I might saunter over to a colleague's cubicle with a question or ask someone to take a quick listen to something I was working on at my desk. Sure,

I could set up a phone call or virtual session or send a Slack message, but it was much less spontaneous and more time consuming, so those moments occurred more infrequently.

Journalists thrive on kibitzing, running a story idea by someone they bump into in the hallway or are standing next to in line while waiting to order their grilled cheese sandwich in the cafeteria. I wonder what brilliant notions or off-the-wall ideas from my co-workers I might have missed out on during lockdown.

And then there is the pal-around factor. I enjoy my colleagues, and there is great camaraderie among the *Weekend* staff. We could still pull off some of that in our virtual editorial meetings, but it hardly measured up to the antics of our in-person sessions.

One or two times a week I did get to go into the office on broadcast days to line-produce the show or edit our podcast *Up First*. Initially, I looked forward to these chances to catch up in person with friends, feel the hum of the newsroom and just sit at my real workspace, as opposed to the spot in our den at home that I shared with our dog Sadie and all the stuffed animals she'd eviscerated.

But the on-site visits quickly became kind of depressing. NPR had turned into a zombie workplace. Two-thirds of the building was shut down, with cordoned-off corridors and locked floors. Just a skeleton crew was allowed to come in, and everyone was, of course, shrouded in masks.

I couldn't go into the studio during the shows to schmooze with Scott or Lulu Garcia-Navarro, and we were spread so far apart in the newsroom that we were forced to yell to each other. And we had to carry around tracking devices that could be used to identify close contacts if a staffer tested positive for the virus.

As I write, NPR is making plans slowly to bring back employees, but there are plenty of people, mostly non-news folks, who will likely never return to the building full time.

Probably the biggest frustration of Covid times for someone like me was the inability to get out in the field to produce and report. NPR didn't want us exposing ourselves to possible infection, so everything had to be done long distance.

Our staff came up with all sorts of innovative ways to keep our programs dynamic, creating signature segments that asked listeners to record themselves with their phones and tell us how Covid had upended their lives or offered them the opportunity to learn how to make sourdough or master three-card monte. But we weren't going anywhere.

A couple of months into lockdown, though, Lulu and I finally got our chance to go into the field. It wasn't far, just down the road really, to Children's National Hospital here in Washington, D.C. At least, it was out of NPR headquarters—and our home office puppy pounds.

We were reporting on MIS-C, multisystem inflammatory syndrome in children, a very rare side effect of Covid in infants and young people that can lead to severe problems with major organs like the heart, lungs or brain. We were the first journalists given access to the pediatric intensive care unit at Children's, which was seeing what doctors there believed to be the most cases of MIS-C in the country.

These were the earliest days of the pandemic, before vaccines, when it wasn't clear just how the virus spread. NPR was figuring out hygiene protocols on the fly. Lulu and I wore masks and face shields and I attached my mic to a telescoping fish pole, so we were able to keep a safe distance from interviewees. I even had to put a condom (non-lubricated) on the mic that could be instantly snapped off and disposed of once we were done.

When I got home, I had to clean my recording equipment with alcohol wipes, strip down before entering my house and immediately toss my clothing in the wash. All of this seemed pretty familiar after my experience with Ebola in Africa.

This assignment was also difficult because of the little victims on whom we were reporting. One baby we observed in intensive care was only six weeks old and hooked up to an array of life-support devices.

A terrified parent looked on from the bedside as their child was kept alive by whirring machines. It was wrenching.

The doctors and nurses we met were heroic and determined to save these kids, working weeks and weeks without a day off. One doctor hadn't seen his family in almost three months. All of the children they were treating would eventually recover, but possible long-term damage to their hearts or lungs may not become evident for decades.

We felt it was crucial to bring attention to this under-covered corner of the Covid story, and Lulu and I won an award for our reporting. This was especially gratifying for me, as MIS-C ended up being the final field piece I would produce as an NPR employee.

# Chapter 37

# Signing Off

Covid helped convince me that the idea of retiring from my only adult job (I practically went from cutting lawns to working at NPR), which I had been harboring for a while, was the right one. Yes, the stories we were covering were critically important, and we were helping our listeners make sense of the pandemic, political divisiveness, and the latest round of culture wars. But working from home, cut off from colleagues without the opportunity to go out in the field was not about to end anytime soon.

Even prior to Covid, plum assignments for me were becoming too few and far between. To be honest, life at NPR had started to feel a bit uncomfortable for an older white guy with a sometimes less than politically correct brand of humor. I started having to be just too careful with my irreverent jokes. I was having less fun.

Ultimately though, I didn't want somebody from the cleaning crew to slurp up my desiccated remains in my cubicle one night when they were vacuuming.

In the ensuing months since retirement, I have missed my colleagues, but not much of the weekly grind. When news breaks on a Friday night, I breathe a sigh of relief that I don't have to figure out how to cover it. Although I have to admit, the Russian invasion of Ukraine inflamed my field-producing genes.

Covid turned all NPR retirements into Zoom events, and I was somewhat dreading mine. I had been to a couple that had their awkward moments as attendees waited for someone to say something nice about the soon to be departed. What if only four people signed on to the call?

As it turned out, lots of people Zoomed in and I was really touched by some of the things folks had to say. I felt a little bit like Tom Sawyer overhearing all those nice comments when he attended his own funeral. This was also the case with some of the emails I got, especially from younger staffers who thanked me for my mentorship, which I honestly hadn't realized I'd provided. As a matter of fact, I always felt I wasn't giving back enough.

On my final day, after my last hours producing *WeSat*, my eyes grew misty as I packed up my cubicle. I was all by myself on the Covid-cleared-out fourth floor of NPR—taking down photos of my daughters as little girls and now as young women about to be college seniors; packing up decades of press passes showing my transformation from bearded long-dark-haired young man to silver thinning-haired crank.

There was a host of other things as well: a charcoal rendering of Muddy Waters drawn for me by one of my students (I teach a college course in audio journalism); my certificate for completing Hostile Environment Training; maps from Luanda, Baghdad, Hanoi, Rwanda, Sudan, Yugoslavia and Afghanistan.

There were also the dozens of manilla folders and reporter's notebooks containing so much research: from stories about Mexican drug cartels; Syrian refugees; Hurricane Katrina; the Rwandan genocide; building implosions; the world's hottest peppers; the world's smallest bird; Cuban cigar rollers; ancient jokes; the Silk Road; the astronaut training program; Indian jumping ants; Biosphere 2; avalanche survivors; dirt bike riders in Baltimore; Mormons in Mexico; a stuntwoman in Hollywood; the U.S. Border Patrol; the 100th anniversary of the Brooklyn Bridge; the 50th anniversary of the end of World War II; the 20th anniversary of *Dr. Strangelove* (We love our anniversaries in public radio); Norman Bates and *Psycho*; and enough blues musicians to fill the entire Mississippi Delta. Yes, I considered all things. Those files all now sit in my basement, too close, probably, to the furnace.

In my final minutes as an NPR employee, I started carting crates with this stuff down to my car in the building garage. But when I walked back up to the security desk and tried to buzz myself back in for a second load, my pass card had already been terminated. Seriously? Talk about a swift kick in the butt. I persuaded the guards to let me through so that I could finish up.

Earlier, that day's show had concluded with a heartfelt on-air tribute to me by Scott. It began with tape of me blowing my harmonica, accompanied by Sadie's howling, and ended, to my absolute chagrin, with more music; but this time it was me playing harp and singing a verse from an original birthday blues I'd recorded for my wife.

Before they hit the tape, the staff invited me into the control room. When the piece was over, a weepy Scott Simon came out of the studio and gave me a big hug. We were all verklempt.

My slow fade to black culminated with a staff party in Scott's apartment. It was the first time we had all been together since before the Covid lockdown the previous year. It felt great. Among my goodbye gifts from *Weekend Edition* was a harmonica case stocked with a full complement of instruments.

Scott also had a literary surprise. For years, he would wander over to my desk at work and present me with copies of books sent to him by publicists which he would then "inscribe"—titles such as *Hitler Was My Neighbor*, with a dedication reading something like, "Dear Peter, Adolf was a better friend than you'll ever be," or *The History of the Wooden Door* with "Peter, always keep your hinges well-oiled."

For my going away party, he presented me a shopping bag full of absurdly-inscribed volumes that he pulled out and read aloud one by one as the goodbye party guests started getting more and more fidgety. Finally, there at the bottom of the bag was an actual gem, a first edition of *No Latitude for Error* by Sir Edmund Hilary, an account of the Mt. Everest hero's traverse by tractor across Antarctica. Of course, Scott couldn't resist an inscription:

**Dear Peter,**
**Eat my snow,**

**—Ed**

PS I'm dead, but still sign books.

The party also included another audio tribute, but this one featured clips from some of the best and worst stories I'd ever produced, along with some sly commentary astutely noting that given all the exotic places I had visited as a reporter and producer, NPR had obviously paid for more than a few of Peter Breslow's summer vacations. Busted!

Oh, and how could I forget—Scott got me a bidet attachment for my toilet from Hellotushy.com.

Enough about me. I think it's time we wrap up this compendium of Breslow arcana, don't you? I will leave you, dear reader, with the goodbye note I sent to NPR staff.

> When I first washed up on National Public Radio's doorstep (The Great Hackensack Calamity of '82) at age 11—I never imagined that all these decades later I would still be at it. It's been quite a run—first at *ATC*—then *Weekend Edition*. Now it's time to say goodbye.
>
> As I grew into long pants, NPR grew as well, from a niche listening experience to the envy of all news organizations, broadcast and otherwise. The cachet that comes with saying I work for NPR is something to cherish.
>
> The work—at times—has been stupendous. Over the years, NPR has sent me on assignment to the highest point on earth (Mt. Everest) to the lowest (the Dead Sea) to the ends of the earth (the South Pole) and lots of spots in between. Along the way, I've gotten to work with a wondrous crew of hosts, reporters, producers, editors, techs—and yes—even managers. (I was actually one for a while.)
>
> There are way too many of them to thank individually in this space, but how can I not raise a virtual glass to the person with whom I have spent the most hours of my adult life (no, not my wife Jessica who I met here)—Scott Simon, certainly the only journalist with whom I've shared a war zone who would stick a pocket square into his Kevlar vest. One day our cache of email exchanges will likely land us both in a federal supermax facility.

You are all the most dedicated, passionate, smartest and, on occasion, best dressed people with whom a former soda jerk at *Breslow's Luncheonette* could ever hope to work. I will especially miss the belly laughs I share weekly with my ultra-talented *Weekend Edition* teammates, who crank it out like fiends every Saturday and Sunday. I stand in awe of you all and know I leave this place in very good hands. I am so sad the pandemic has kept us apart my final year.

I will continue teaching, playing the blues, riding my bike and, of course, carving championship wooden duck decoys. I've also got a memoir I'm finishing.

I'd hug you if I could . . .

—Peter

Oh wait, I'm not quite finished. Let the record show that the very next morning after my final day producing *WeSat*, NPR suffered a catastrophic meltdown of all its audio and editorial systems that nearly knocked the network off the air. I am told that during the havoc that day a cry went out through the newsroom—*Breslow is to blame!*

My work is done here. And so, for one last time . . .

*This is Peter Breslow, NPR News.*

Mic drop

## AUTHOR'S NOTE

This is a memoir. I have tried my very best to faithfully portray people, places and events as honestly as I can recall them. But, hey, some of this stuff happened a long time ago. Some quotes may not be exact, though their sensibility certainly is. If details of an occasion are not absolutely precise, they are pretty darn close and do not alter the story appreciably. There may be a bit of artistic license here and there to help the narrative flow. That said, I do have a pretty good memory. Just ask what's his name.

Thanks for reading this thing. It didn't take very long, did it? If you enjoyed the experience, could you please leave a somewhat positive review at your online bookstore, Goodreads, BookBub or on your social media platform of choice. And if you invite me to your book club, I promise I will make chocolate egg creams for everyone—I still remember how.

## AND FROM NPR

The views and opinions expressed in this book are those of the author and do not necessarily reflect any official policies or positions of National Public Radio, Inc.

## ACKNOWLEDGMENTS

There is a lifetime of people to thank when you write a memoir, but that's probably a few too many to list here, so I'll narrow it down.

Thanks and more thanks to novelist, teaching colleague and friend, Professor Steven Hayward who pushed me to write this book and extended a strong editorial hand; and to Book Doctor Arielle Eckstut who (with David Sterry) offered so much guidance from the title to getting this thing into print.

I am also grateful to my early readers Stefanie Wallach, Art Silverman, John Ydstie, Terrel Lamb, Judi Goodstein and Anne Goodwin Sides for their spot-on suggestions.

Great appreciation to Sammi Eckstut for her keen-eyed copy editing and Mark Melnick for his deft book design; and Kim Weiss and Eva Natiello for promotion help.

High fives to collaborators who became buddies over the years: David Sheff, A.J. Jacobs, Hampton Sides, Jim Robbins; and to Everest teammate Doug Burbank for his details about our time on the mountain.

Hats off to my many friends who have heard every one of these stories at least 47 times and smile patiently as I tell them yet again: Fionnuala Conway, Guy Slattery and Landy Slattery (for their book design advice too), Russell Wallach, Shannon Murphy, David Murphy, Cecile Heron, Nick Heron, Cynthia Baker, Jon Zeitler, Diana Blitz, John Copacino, Maddy Beckwith and John Grint; and especially Jersey Boys Mark Devlin, Chris Buri, David Lefty Monahan, Mike Palermo, Mike Padua and Gary Folley; and to bike riding sidekick Jim Werner.

I owe a huge debt to all the NPR producers, editors, hosts, reporters, managers, techs, researchers and fixers who over the decades assisted, corrected and inspired me. It is impossible to name them all but a scattershot sampling includes (and apologies to those I've omitted): Susan Stamberg, Scott Simon, Lulu Garcia-Navarro, Rachel Martin, Sarah Oliver, Evie Stone, Ned Wharton, Samantha Balaban, Barrie Hardymon, Ed McNulty, Melissa Gray, Ian Stewart, Hiba Ahmad, Hadeel al-Shalchi, D. Parvaz, Andrew Craig, John Burnett, Robert Siegel, Renee Montagne, Liane Hansen, Don Gonyea, Tom Bowman, Melissa Block, John Nielsen, Tom Gjelten, Michael Sullivan, Alex Chadwick, Linda Wertheimer, Daniel Zwerdling, Jim Kane, Chuck Holmes, Noah Adams, Deb Amos, Jacki Lyden, Zalmai Yawar, Shafi Sharifi, Kee Malesky, Gwen Thompkins, Cindy Carpien, Darcy Bacon, Les Cook, Alice Winkler, Rebecca Davis, Al Letson, David Welna, Carrie Kahn, Tom Goldman, John Ogulnik, Julie McCarthy, Steven Reiner, Ted Clark, Richard Harris, Jay Kernis, Bob Duncan, Bill Buzenberg, Marcus Rosenbaum, Leo del Aguila, Stu Rushfield, Manoli Wetherell, Flawn Williams, Marty Kurcias and Suraya Mohamed.

In memoriam: Neal Conan, Mike Shuster, Daniel Schorr, Jim Angle, Anne Garrels, Duc Nguyen, Carolyn Jensen Chadwick and David Gilkey.

Love to my parents, Dave and Sari Breslow, who loved their kids and tried the best they could; and to my dear sisters Linda Kreisel and Susie Rakusin, who looked out for their little brother (and still do); and to the rest of the mishpucha inner circle: Bruce Rakusin, Suzanne Goldstein, Noah Goldstein, Jenny Michaelson, Wenderson Leandro De Paula, and dearly departed Ted Goldstein.

And limitless love to my astounding family—Jessica Goldstein, Danielle Anna Breslow and Eden Rose Breslow. You are my greatest story and adventure.

Made in the USA
Las Vegas, NV
04 January 2024

83914849R00121